Collected Poems

of

Richard Alan Bunch

1965-2011

∞INFINITY
PUBLISHING

Copyright © 2011 by Richard Alan Bunch

ISBN 0-7414-6763-1

Printed in the United States of America

This is a work of fiction. Names, characters, places, and incidents either are the product of the author's imagination or are used fictitiously. Any resemblance to actual events or locales or persons, living or dead, is entirely coincidental.

Published August 2011

INFINITY PUBLISHING
1094 New DeHaven Street, Suite 100
West Conshohocken, PA 19428-2713
Toll-free (877) BUY BOOK
Local Phone (610) 941-9999
Fax (610) 941-9959
Info@buybooksontheweb.com
www.buybooksontheweb.com

Richard Alan Bunch

Collected Poems
1965-2011

Vincennes University
Shake Learning Resources Center
Vincennes, In 47591-9986

To the memory of my parents

and to

Rita, Katie, and Ricky

Preface

Throughout this work, from traditional to experimental, the reader will notice continuing experiments with language, voice, imagery, form, diction, rhythm, and so forth. Welcome to these language-experiments, my poems.

Grateful acknowledgment is made to the following editors and publishers in whose publications (including online) earlier or final versions of some of these poems first appeared: *Slant, Journal of Contemporary Anglo-Scandinavian Poetry, Splizz, Brownstone Review, Sonoma Mandala, New Thought Journal, Many Mountains Moving, Candelabrum Poetry Magazine, Blue Heron Quarterly of Haiku and Zen Poetry, Spokes, Enigma, Presence, Porcupine Literary Arts Journal, Fire, Black Mountain Review, Mandrake Poetry Magazine, Vanderbilt Divinity Review, The Plaza, West Wind Review, Kinesis, Cold Mountain Review, Black Moon, Amber, Xavier Review, Axe Factory Review, Avocet, Snakeskin Anthology, Fugue, Tucumcari Literary Review, Veil, Old Red Kimono, Hawai'i Review, Coracle, Sivullinen, Long Islander, 42opus, Poetry Nottingham, Green's Magazine, Footprints, Open Bone, Red Cedar Review, The Alembic, Lucid Stone, Japanophile, Comstock Review, Iconoclast, Caveat Lector, Lucid Moon, Studio One, Orphic Lute, NeoVictorian/Cochlea, Green Fuse, Chaminade Literary Review, Mind in Motion, Wiseblood, Butterfly Chronicles, Takahe, Roanoke Review, The Cape Rock, Nebo, MM Review, Listening Eye, Orbis, Mañana, Idiom 23, Albatross, Paper Salad Poetry Review, Midwest Poetry Review, Coe Review, Ginger Hill, Offerte Speciale, The Journal* (U.K.), *Windsor Review, Konfluence, Heliotrope, Studio, Northwest Florida Review, Acid Angel, Newsletter Inago, Prairie Winds, Poetry New Zealand, Here's To Humanity 2000, Goose River Anthology, Alternative Arts and Literature Magazine, Kimera, James River Poetry Review, Angel Face, Poetry Midwest, California Quarterly, Poetry Depth Quarterly, Maelstrom, The New Formalist, Potpourri, European Judaism, Zillah, Raintown Review, In A Family Way Anthology, Poet's Haven, Haight Ashbury Literary Journal, Jessamyn West Review, American Poets and Poetry, Dry Bones Anthology 2000, Oregon Review, Quercus Review, Dirigible, Poetic Voices Journal, Sacred Journey, Rockhurst Review, Spindrift,*

Mid-America Poetry Review, A Stone's Throw Anthology,
Poetry Cornwall, Tule Review, Poetic Eloquence, Ilya's Honey,
Poetry Now, Chaffin Journal, Napa Valley Artscan, Ruah V,
Latino Stuff Review, Dan River Anthology, Night Roses,
Riverrun, Timber Creek Review, Talvpaivanseisaus Specials,
Pudding House Publications Anthology, The Tomcat, Artemis,
Opus Literary Review, The Scribbler, Homestead Review,
Sulphur River Literary Review, Affair of The Mind, Pinyon,
The Lamp-Post, Gryphon, Kennesaw Review, Lalitamba,
Twilight Ending, Northern Stars Magazine, The Magpie's Nest,
Hidden Oak Poetry Journal, Poetalk, Three Cup Morning,
Pebble Lake Review, The Gathering, Owen Wister Review,
Wavelength, Songs of Experience, River Poets Journal,
Sierra Nevada College Review, Carpe Laureate Diem, Promise,
Beyond Doggerel, Grasslands Review, Quantum Leap, Poesia,
Pegasus, Thorny Locust, Speedpoets, Thoughts for all Seasons,
The Pinehurst Journal, Red Owl Magazine, Afterthoughts,
Voices International, Suisun Valley Review, Lilliput Review,
Hazmat Review, White Wall Review, River Oak Review,
Skyline Magazine, Cherry Blossom Review, New Contrast,
Napa Valley College Academic Senate Journal, Enclave,
Meridian Anthology of Contemporary Poetry, A Hudson View,
Hurricane Review, Tipton Poetry Journal, Poetry Midwest,
Red River Review, Poetry Repairs, Sepia, Poetry Southeast,
Wild Goose Poetry Review, Literary House Review, Nexus,
Raintown Review, Poets Express, Wild Violet, Poetry Vibes,
Curriculum Vitae Literary Supplement, short poems, The Oak,
Burning Cloud Review, Epicenter, Wings, Orphic Lute,
Bay Area Poets Coalition, Ancient Pathways, Poetic License,
Language and Culture Review, Mermaid Tavern Anthology,
Sun Poetic Times, Journeys of the Mind, Defiance!, The Quest,
Poem, New Mirage Quarterly, Mandrake Poetry Review,
Concrete Wolf, The Heron's Nest, Plain Spoke, Book of Hopes
and Dreams Anthology, and Brobdingnagian Times.

Contents

Mozart by the Sea

With green vision she attends to Mozart's
Eine Kleine Nachtmusik, that dark art,
And feels it woven with fresh-fathered seas,
Breathes its beats as her heart bears repeating.
A whole note's but a quarter of her past—
This keeps her married to the summer grass.
She recalls how rhythm can ripen, compose
To apocalypse and how Mozart flows
As natural as breakers breaking to
Sunrise with a looking-glass. In this mood
She beholds a blue sensuousness, a
Cascade of sound, seas that season both ways
Sound keeps feeding, reflects, and weighs her soul
And makes listening fields, the world's blood, show.

The Daffodil in Apogee

As the bay
turns
toward the setting sea
the fog
with its charcoal-calibrated elbows
its reddish brown odors
of cod and yellow fish
stands
as the rememberer
in winds
that warn and prance
and with a spidery movement
leans
like a dreamer's text
into your yellow darkening
distancing
field.

Santa Rosa Plums

My father's ardor, the grafting art,
that budding genealogy of God's delight.
The loving pear's archetypal music,
apple's thoughtless geography,
the wild plum's wilder loins,
a family pigmented with longing.

He stood there in a gray sweatshirt,
old khaki pants, shoes full
of holes, and cut off a pair of
limbs to make a new one.

Then he sliced further down
that soul's anatomy, pried it
open for a virginal smile,
a newer shoot, the Santa Rosa
plum, the ones that redden
deeper with each passing summer's skin.

Strips of bedsheets held
the shoots together. Daubing hot pitch,
he watched as these strange new lovers
dried a dripping black. Once cooled, he relit
his pipe, grinned, and moved the ladder closer to heaven.

His ardor was hard to resist. In fusion,
he knew, scars were never certain.
They could cleave like politics.

Being and Having
(after Gabriel Marcel)

Having it all
was the way we were tried,
a spectacle of foreign display,

2

the way having was supposed by pundits
to be of the same groundwork as being
but is, instead, a thousand lives away.

Too little
did we love ourselves
for who we were
in breath and bone and blood.

Too long
did we love a plastic image of ourselves
lost in the unthinking shuttle
among boatloads of the dead.

Milton's Muse

I have lost my socks to Milton's muse
And found my tissues in nets of hills
Where sunsets dance in flaming shoes
And burning oak in an ageless well.

I have lost my pants to Milton's muse
And thunder my child in drowsy blood
Where twilight lovers snake in the blues
And mellow within the pulse of drums.

I have lost my ties to Milton's muse
Who rankles time with an inch of leaves
And offers homage to veins of mood
And yanks yogis from the bartered earth.

The Edge

You have to be keenly aware
of the axe which smells of fur
and blood. You've deluded yourself

into thinking
they won't get rid of you
that you've worked so hard and so well
that nothing like this could happen
to you.

And then one fine day (or night
if they're especially nasty)
you discover we all dangle
in separate skins.
Older blood divorces.
Edges of cordiality
suddenly fold
into stone. Some
friends turn out to be
stillborn after all.

You cringe as you hear the good news.
First your titles, your keys,
next your name, your face,
what little urn of space you occupied,
your worth in money and performance
gone.

You think you've become a dismembered dog
with no opportunity.

It's then that you begin to realize the vast ocean
of the toilet
you've been treading
all these years.

Then it is time for Zen. You remember
the story. Chased by a ravenous tiger
who aches to eat him,
a man finds himself
hanging over a cliff by two vines

4

being eaten by three mice.
Below, starved lions
wait to devour him.
While hanging, he sees
a wild strawberry. He plucks
and eats it. And it is
so delicious.

Portraits at Summer Solstice

1.

The young girl colors a picture of the Hotel Milano.
In front by the steps the Virgin Mary is shown in a burning
bush. She senses rainbows need a vineyard.

2.

In his Japanese garden, a gesture of manna,
the veteran cultivates shadows in pools, quarries.

3.

"Look. There's snow on the mountains. In summer,"
he says, "let's eat watermelons." She says:
"The lake is too cold. Glaciers do not melt even now."

4.

She paints a vine branch an autumn deeper red,
sensing anthropology begins in trees.

5.

Beachcombing for hungry tigers, he encounters tide pools
and salmon-colored islands thick as stars. Fishing syntaxes,
coagulating guilt, camps of snow that yield cults of fiction.

Below granite-slabbed cliffs, he sees through the currents
starfish holding on in their hunger.

6.

"The infinite in art," he says holding virgin olive oil, "includes
the summer of experience, the flesh of the August plum."

7.

She says "I didn't know you had it in you." At the time she
mused he was just another loser, a bitter saying of her great
aunt in Toronto. "I do," he said, as he continued drawing his
journey eastward. It was his summer solstice, a circled ring he
used to renounce her world steeped in the sestinas of common
sense. "I knew I would," he confessed, returning to his original
design.

8.

In the picture she notices temptation in pastels: date palms and
ferns, throats lingering for an idea, horses in the shape of an
altarpiece, evil without end, wrists of sandstone, umbrellas
turned oracles that suggest a human thaw.

9.

He runs his hand through the shifting waters.
In the widening light she keeps growing.

10.

"Fans cool me," she says, as beams crack, the air singes,
skies loom assertive opal. She watches him in the flowers.
Colors burst alive, ignite raw awakenings.

Leonardo's Eye

In your book of sketches, helicopters
shadow the deltoids of fresh cadavers or
chins that jut from sunny villas
where no nuns roam, the grime
of the Etruscan vanquished, born
into the thrownness of circumstance.

Like many, you're possessed
by the magna vox of classic vision,
the engineering ear, bridges
that lift the despairing into
philosophy. Stamens of the eye
unfold for you like submarines

of a future's shrinking calm.
A botanist, you blend *chiaroscuro*
with the swift in flame, geometries
with balanced hands. In your book
of sketches the future of war maps
fabrications of another generation's

truth. With you, boundaries appear
to vanish. Yours the price of
genius with each *sfumato* stroke.

The Dictionary of Music

In the dictionary of music
    there are parent countries
that deploy tonal tactics
    on a major scale.

Songs of the bodiless finally enflesh,
    scale yesterday's
afflictions like ghosts of forget-me-nots,
    halos of an arctic sun,

spirit swelled past the temptations of artifice.

Beneath the dictionary of music
   there are invisible harmonies,
plots that play more than episodes,
alloys of poetry,
    birds of paradise that canonize the motherland.
Here domains modulate to the right angle
   range fireballs around a madrigal in coiled codas.

Atop the dictionary of music
   ballerinas play panpipes,
bluebells gain passports
   to make history timeless,
flugelhorns become blazing stars,
   suspended cymbals
polarized by exile, romance the tropical
   in bones of mist
as blue bouzoukis thrum vibrations of emptiness
   and find it luminous.

First Fish

Circular to the last, you can retrieve the first.
Imagine lips parted as though to resort to chemistry

As you troll a virgin river without end.
The lines at first seem endless. Then other tests

At twenty, fifty, and eighty, each stress
accents a new catch on another's line.

Matters soon taste all-too-human, assume
A visible diction—bass, pike, sunfish—shades of an ancient name.

Imperceptibly it becomes harder to snag that first one.
You can retrieve simplicity, the way your first hook,

Hallowed by the everyday, is struck with new luster.

Imagine trolling the river of those departed. How tunnels
At both ends light, hook of that eye first opening.

Among Others Night Is Just One

Orchards pruned dot the yellowed hills
On a morning now genderless in fog.

Vineyards replay their oaths of solitude,
Ripen to the flights of birds.

The stars engender hope without boundaries
Then fade in a sleep of their past lights.

"Bring me into your dreams," she says.
I open my arms, beckon the way a miracle does.

Spiders

Daughters
of night, they spin, weave
and snip destinies of silk.

Each strand the lot
for some suspecting morsel
who crawls or slides or stumbles
into this fellowship of hunger.

Those arms seem so weak
but hold up the gun and the gun's wife,
accent the perishing, and blind those
who yearn to leave
this company of the gods.

These sisters live
to weave, to span the lines.

Someday they might
just stitch this loved earth,
this body's bride, into
winter roses made of silk.

To a Friend Nursing a "Beyond Death" Experience

Horizons are bandits, you say,
Resting half mad in the eastern rain,
That we here are dreamers of fury,
Victims of angst,
Thighs of our vulnerable maybes.

The certitude in your voice and your gait
Concerns me.
You say that roofless silence,
That swallow of the summits,
Carries the day, that there's no fear in journeys
Of the spirit,
Manifestoes of the sun,
In putting out, in the last of earth,
That there's more beauty in the laughter
Waking over there.

It is not for me to parade,
Sometimes in unwitting dress,
Upon your solitudes, the heart of your reach
Of constant fire,
Those sprinkling sands of staging a comeback.
I have my own paradoxes to live,
My pangs, with all their wintry diamonds, to die.

Enchantments

By sheer survival, the moon suggests
the classical, sometimes
being outshone by the range
of choices, and in repeated exposures
grows passive, a deflated stranger
in a mantra of aloneness
though cast always young
to the resurgent core.

Through a magical arithmetic,
a global collage, that
anachronism
called in theory the present,
hauntingly postmodern, nearly comic
(if not ironic) the moon's
texture confesses
(and supposedly empties)
that complexion's reflection
from a text without a context.
But such misses the conception
between fold upon brooding
fold, through interstitial
tissues of rain, sun and
wild wind in season
and out when
the moon still pours
a softer light
into those uncut futures,
the heartshapes
of childhood, a light
older than that sound of oars
dipped by the crew of Ulysses
into open sea, more prehistoric
than art carved on the walls of caves
that engenders vision,
nakedly young, organic.

Sky Blue

Can you finger that skyey
riot come of age with frost, mountains
furrowed, the tympanics of spring?

The hymns, thrums abuzz
with mustard-deep illuminations
unplucked from April's fields,
and still stroke the central sound,
tip the primordial wine?

Listen. Explode the now
with a delicious silence
to forge beyond blood-bred twilights,
bellow past the smoking dragons
brow-deep, atom-steeped in ideologies.
For the end sky drums the bluest blue.

The Uprooted Baskets at Ridgeview Jr. High

(for Jim Herrman)
Mais ou sont les neiges d'antan?
—François Villon

Saturday mornings those mouth-shaped hoops
would be there, overnight, still, open
to hold the passing air as though to suspend
                    us.
Our bikes were parked like a private
audience, a source of solitudinous cheers.

First warm-ups: jumpers, sky hooks,
butterflies in slow motion. Soon we'd
get our "eye," take sides and strides
in sync, a half-court show. Fakes,
dribbles, pivots, dunks, the swishing ends
always the same—

pure ice cream.

But those plays are gone. Perhaps
we outgrew that stage. Only gray
patches remain, skeletons of another season,
containing moves only now to be
imagined.

At the Home for Veterans

                      Stonehenge still,
in the likenesses of no other love, the veterans
                  grappling with
the mold of their age, doze. One sleeps in
a wheelchair wrapped in a plastic tube that snakes
and spans a fitful neck around which hangs
the *Croix de Paix.* Another leans
forward as though she's posed or
poised to hear someone rave orders from tomorrow's
field that was once a touching past completely
out of bloodless martial hearing.

                    Still another's cane
rests against his inner seam. A tube huddles around the tag that
names him, a parenthesis
that argues into a void. His dreams no longer seem
                  to complete the art of war—
now he marshals the sun's missiles into his eye.

                    Just then a coin
plunks down the vending machine's rust-free throat.

Someone in white
                  with a loyalist hand

removes one Dr. Pepper. As they slumber with a foreign war's
sound, the TV

                              fractures
intensities of their snores, dances its war games
                            just this side
of human darkness.

Seawind in the Plums

This evening
ruffles of surf
draw out shrinking sand.

Casts of the sea pull us.

Holding you here
the rustle of your dress
seawind in the plums
the moon's cupped light.

We touch
what a wave marks-
that small world
flared up like split bone.

The sound of sound
resounding of surf
opens us
far beyond
that glib theater of the brain.
Hypnotic sea-veins
emerald fists
pull and pull
until we fast become
the underside
beauty between us.

Fort Ross in Early Spring

A white house sits washed
On a green hill blurred by wisps of certainty.

Here and there lilies in a heart-answering cluster
Dance wild with yellow remembrance.

Odors thick with eucalyptus mingle
With submarine grasses.

In its black and white designs a heron stares seaward
As a brown mare grazes and smells of unsaddled lust.
Gulls and whitecaps in syncopation mark the season's erosion
Burnt with the texture of a fever's onrush.

One grey gull persists, lonely on a rock in spindrift,
Amid the misty jazz of saltwater.

Listening to the cove below
Waves lap and return, return and lap,

The beach awash with sand-bubbly things
And the disclosive stages of God.

Picnickers weathering this symphonic poem
Abide within abide without, eating and eaten.

    Jays hop in campfire ashes
    Chipmunks play on granite
    Stars appear.

    among yellow stamens
    and this salmon sunset—
    a swan's head

A Man for No Seasons

One. An ancient theme. A thinker
Who, by equations of midnight, finds
Polaris by daylight. An Aleph.

Crystalline, pure, a philosopher of the gaze,
His light blinds unholy diamonds. His
Reflections rain azaleas, upgather homemade cemeteries.

Through the arrow of desire there's a divine sunbreaking,
The alpha who does not end by spinning
Pearls of glass.

Transubstantiation in Blue

yes as lovers we flow
to the sounding sea
poundings the sea hallows
the ever sun-brided sea
you rising out of the me
of me you pine for
in the sunshivering sea
the elements you pine for
in the sea of me

we lovers school the sea
flushed with rebirth
communing loins like
plucked ganders of foam
you can rise from the illusion
of me like mendicants burning
to deep kiss the holy noon

we lovers go to
the resounding sea
in a schooner of souls

herdings past history's
fume and rack
and again you rise
out of the sea of me
with no illusions
of fireless voices
or the politics of hollow eyes

we lovers school the sea
in threshed enskyment
in madness and sad guitars
in summits of unshouldered beauty
in drums of brokered eyelids
connoisseurs of sunslips and slapsilver
we lovers school the sea

Flights of Wild Geese

Those black necks
    stretch through clouds
as though to rekindle
    desire
from the ashes, seeking you out
    like love
long gone, now come home.
    Far away
they seemed penciled
    eyebrows
dateless dates, mere
    names lost
in the winnowing. A green
    lake chalice
beckons. Charcoal webs,
    wings thunderous
gather in slow motion
    a descent
to replay those untried

promises
silent as the swarming
   of desire.
A plumose carpet sways
   the ripples.
This is only a sabbath
   in their
graceful sweep. Like
   morning mists
that rise from summer
   waters, they shall
resume the stretch
   and fly to
turn old blood over
   down wind.

Brief Bios

1.

Mary lived to bury her sisters and died
bite by bite by the sheer loss of earth.

2.

With paparazzi in pursuit, Farnsworth rolled
in silver wheels until his soul cost more than his billions.

3.

When rats his paper windows, Odie felt
his bludgeoned soul decry the pain of poverty.

4.

At ninety-eight, Elizabeth the bread maker
had broken her share. Pundits applauded.

5.

Cradling the sky, Horace put his thumb
through a dipper of stars.

Mates

Death's opening moves are classic:
He always takes your horse.

The Queen is not much help. She
Snorts cocaine and rocks
Her flesh to sleep.

The King also tries escape,
His castle of balloons.

A winter's orchestra,
Death's hand moves knights ahead
Of the bishop's mirth.

There's a pallbearer in love's snow.
Angels rest adrift. And death
Smiles into the next century.

The King keeps running in his tennis
Whites and hides in his castled self.
He confesses he is thinner than the
Hiss of desire, the pianos of night.

Death coughs, under the weather.
He too is persistent. And perishes
In the artful possibility
That you may not exist.

The Compleat Anglers
(after Izaak Walton)

Wind claws water
With a simple faith in abiding silence.

Pines circle pines
Whenever a bluegill or rainbow rises.

Ducks search treetops for a skein
Of wild geese in flight

As skies sheep-mellowed on a lost wisdom
Fleck deepening water.

Fish diving underground awaken
The magic hearse.

Water splicing mind carries its master
Down to a purple sea.

Trees scissoring sky
Rip through jaded confessions

While butterflies eluding age
Undress summer beneath a trout-swirled fog.

Fog

A way of finding yourself
lost where fog clings. Veins of
remembered playlight begin to blur.

Steady heart, wave battalions
pound and blast. You cannot see
them, only savor a restlessness
that whomps as April's blood.

Who you are erases here like a native
earth present in unseen praise.
Masks of rock jut out beyond
the sea and sadness.

Like the you
you once thought you were
they appear to accept this orchestration,
a reminder that fogscapes
are the mind's deadly poem, those
questioning streets
borne in difference.

Running for Daybreak

Stretched beyond horizons of breath
Those muscles pound into the beach's strand.

The sun unveils breathlessly on water
Like rain-filled willows that branch into spring.

Combing waves mark the shore and sultrier markets:
Sweat beads your shoulders row on thirsting rows.

Ahead, stars await behind a forgotten moon.
Daylight fritters vermilion and poppy on its way south.

As that breathing slows, the pace begins to go.
You need another light to get through this night

To remember there are ways to be still
In the sometimes nowhere of all this commotion.

Endgame

I see that inner fire
That makes angels of dried bones

In deserts where you ride this stallion
Across miles and miles of naked soul.

I hear your love slow down and die
In those unresolved confessions
Dying into death's sudden song
And still in some way you resurrect
All that weaves us as earth.
I watch the love you call love
Become winters of familiar fits
And wear out in drifts of unnatural light
Our tomorrows try to feverishly forget.
You try in every love to find
Love that is blind, in front, below, divine.

The love you love vanishes
Demands those remains of you
You cannot unearth to share.
So you replay the search, the craving, the dying
For the love that empties with every love.

The Liliuokalani Gardens

A rainless afternoon, windward Hilo.
Watching her kids
A woman in a blue-flowered kimono munches coleslaw.
Golden-red fish patrol the ponds, scavenge food
From all of us passersby.

Pagodas sentinel next to sculpted gray lions.
A torii gate separates sacred
From profane space.
In the distance of Shinto myth
The primal creator couple
Izanagi flees Izanami
In the land of the dead.

Coconut palm fronds rub
Their rosin in crinkly flutters.
Undulations wash the shores of Hilo Bay
Lined with fishermen.

We have come for a picnic.
Between gates we pause to listen
To the banyan tree blend of Hawai'i
And the land of the rising sun.

Steinbeck Country

To the east, the Gabilan Mountains;
Off to the west, the Santa Lucias.

Then the long Salinas Valley
Where dust riders ride the heat
Dancing into hispanic earth;
Where heads of lettuce green,
Artichokes bear their hearts and
Southern Pacific boxcars couple.

Not far away breakneck whitecaps
Nudge those unhurried odors
Of Monterey and Cannery Row.

Up the peninsula, at Stanford's farm,
The studied biology of an unstable earth.

Unveiling

We kiss beneath white wild stars
and open this earthly summer.

For so long I have surrendered
myself to random joys
like a sleepwalker

who fears her darker wisdoms,
her deftly-stitched bounds
between earthbound need
and castblind wish.

No longer.
Your eyes in mine
bloom into attar sloops of wind.

Memories burning with you
will upturn more bliss
than any marriage
in the mouth.

With you I will no longer reminisce
the future and its lidless griefs.

Yielding Our Bread

Perhaps memory is what yields
Our bread, our taste for the infinite
Apples that do not end
In the fruit of bitter days
Climbing darkly, darkly
Like roots of darkest night,
Forgotten by habit in the
Narcotic of routine. No, here are
Clearings in the unclearings
Of despair, the kind of day
When you can still
See sails on a turquoise sea.

That taste of remembrance
Rises and slowly ever rises
With a foretaste
So unlike a valley bleached
Dry with broken bones.

The Painted Desert

sunsets aflame
dance
fiercest orange
yielding red
fists of clay

Indian brushes
blush
crimson
thunderstorms
paint
when rain
hammers
those
petaled arms

juniper
bullsnakes
wind-scarped
hills: these
faces too
fold
into silence

Conjunctions

1.

The rabbit's fur drips with rain
beneath the redwoods. In the wood
summer still sleeps.

2.

The sage muses

on the meaning of being
and its disclosive art:
a novel language for the dying.

3.

In a subway station down the eye of a pistol
aging is kinder than winter
contained by the savage heart.

4.

Pearls lying in darker waters
secrete ambition, the prize of
knives. They pry into secret lives.

5.

Canopy of the galaxy, the body's sacred time,
an explosion to lift the blessed,
for all spiritual destinies
in matter begin.

6.

Worms crawl out of apple-dreams
and go back to those unheard refrains,
lineals of the ancestral blood.

7.

Viruses appear at prime time,
once more fusing body with mind,
coiling around our comedy
with the bronze of winter.

Serpents of death
squirm through membranes,
anonymous, double-minded,
shuffling with the odds. They too
enliven biographies of grenadine
amid the driftwood decor.

9.

Heart of sky, heart of earth,
parents of return,
all-too-soon recast
the violin's sound and its tenor,
idioms that implicitly disclose
the spectrum of silence.

Essays in Divinity

> *Cherish in yourself*
> *the birth of God.*
> —Meister Eckhart

> *What is divinity if it can come*
> *Only in silent shadows and in dreams?*
> —Wallace Stevens

My last poem lying in the dark;
the nurse has left.
I feel my breathing heavy, my chest
covered with white hair.
Upon me has fallen the hermeneutic
wonder of dreams. In them, I dance

like Zorba the Greek and love women
only God's love can mystically fashion.

Evenings discover me gazing at lines
etched at the Moulin Rouge by my friend,
Lautrec.

In Athens I discuss particulars of
beauty with Plato who hankers for
souls anchored in stars.

On Lesbos, Sappho takes her girls gently
by the arm and teaches them poetry
deeper than a sigh.

Chaplain motored here this afternoon
espousing Christ and his mystic tide.

She also likes the Buddha's flower sermon
that cuts diamonds made of silk. I would

like to take tea with the lady. She does
not wear her badge like the Pharisees: her

Zen sees too far. Her prayers Om.
There is no room for her love of God.

Dreaming, I see life in other universes
and hear restaurants on the moon within

constellations of light years nearest, a
rainbow's genesis surpassing civilization.
Light stabs as curtains part. The
Physician opens my eyes galloping dream,
another pulse!

Dreams have become more real in this

last testament. What we call reality
can be a supremely fictive will, Madame.
A door softly opens:

I hear Neruda in the next age
savoring a breast of his final rose
eternally in flight.

And Tu Fu's brush concentrates:
sunsets magenta as plums inspire

each stroke higher than a man: ageless
ways words mother the fathered heart.

Nearness of end: even here dreams
clarify this orange evening

when the sun also rises
in the shape of Mexico.

A Gap in Being

When he comes home
    from the trenches, this falling
hostage of myths, nearly erect,
    bloodied, thrown,
a pursuer of wisdom once,
    kindler of scientific futures,
this heroic pose
    oozing now
no longer dances
    in divine wonder.

His wars
    on his kindred
splinter vision,
    mutilate torsos,
ape

his wars on the shrinking earth
leave him with a skull
   fabricated
without a trace
   of the lived sacred.
Is his a passage
   in eclipse,
his island
   a native of nothing;
his genocidal schemes
   what do they make him?
a master of oblivion?

Dictionary of Wars

1.

Our veins drown in autobiography
that résumé of reversals, nuclear
mushrooms, odors of transient flakes.
They gun with smoke the carnage
of misjudgment, chronicled waste.

2.

Some avatars specialize
in death by the numbers:
caesars in miniature who try
double-crossing kingdoms
of the die through genetics and genocide.
"The moon's my mother," they all lie,
"the sun's my twin with legions to prove it."
And those legions are ready
to fleece and be fleeced again.

3.

You ponder the Crimean War
or maybe the Jugurthine.
Or a campaign as real,
the wars of philosophy: a spider's
phenomenal web, the world, spun
out of the One, and how that one finally
finds itself in the twittering of swallows
the timbre and tune of the mother tongue.

4.

Hunters emerge from the woods stalking the inflated
self. They know beatific deer
from an emperor of hunger.
Nor are they surprised at the ascent
of buddhas
prized above tidal remains
of their former selves.
Amazing what you catch when you journey
down   down   down   down
to where the sun sleeps and
slips.

5.

Tail in her mouth a serpent forms
a perfect O
that yoni circle, the unbroken we leave
broken. Dreams burning
for skylight thus rise to erect and
struggle to co-direct the
wakings of sunless seas,
cutthroats with copper looks who bandit
power for power's shrieks
and philosophy's intimate mountains
monologues no less that matter
long after the ends of the ending earth.

6.

Not just seal pups clubbed senseless
their burgundy blood spilled on spikes
of ice. Nor the condor soaring into a
shadow of itself. Nor barnacled whales
that spew out their gunned and
sad narratives. Not just these
but the grey earth itself. And the very air.
Few holy ones are breathing here.

7.

Thrown. And thrown again. As though shot
into this world we arrive in
funereal cars and
throughout this fleshy
night are marked to be veins
of a tolling vine.
Still we're lured by another shore
to become breakers
of the midnight sun
and thus discern the sacred
among the murderous weeds.

8.

Is there no apparent future? Are
history's sutures forever
bound to be
undone?
Strained blanks and passages—
another turn at the gun.

Peeling Off

The way sun spatters, spits past irony
through colored glass, or nightfall darkens a round
stone, or how thumbs when stressed blush by degrees—
these voices all hush when your love's risk has flown
downwind and left blue horses of mourning, leaves
stained sorrow, suns made of coal, bleating breasts,
worms for lips, trombones empty, all. You grieve
and rise and bleed and find in each breath death
another of your arts as death's olde thyme
steals the spice of loss, the retrieves of leaves
and engraves on your lonesome homeless charm
a new-borne will's codicil to bequeath:
you pick up your guts and from this cave go
blossom a burnt wisdom who over-knows.

Windward Oahu

On each horizon ships plod without motion.
Lightning cracks amid spindrift
As energy valences
Map the dance, detail unflagging epiphanies.

Each fathom confesses a shoreless owning.
Foam after form: still at daybreak
The cravings for form, for foam.
In deep breaths, waves *are*
Particles in mindscapes of reef.

Storms invite. Surfaces echo
Wading questions

Where wind and the hands of chance
Husband oceanic pastures of the blood,
Aims of our fragments and fire.

Fisherman from Kolkata

Once an old man arrived in a village far away.
He heard the bickerings through lungs of extremity.

Then he turned to the sun and stared.
He had gone into the sea only to ask why.

"Why do these lovers get caught
On the addiction to this, the id of that?"

He could gaze at the sun for hours
While everyone else learned to panic.

As he bent down and kissed the thudding horses of illusion,
He embraced the drums of peace, his undying every breath.

In him was sea, sky, and land, a promised dedication
To the elusive silence he listened for.

Secret of the Golden Flower

This peace and inward silence
cannot always be explained
whether one fishes the Arafura Sea
or sashays toward Longfellow Peak.
How about purity of heart?

In the clearing bliss of the other shore,
Healing can be uncovered:
In this human family we can learn to love
Leaving infallibility and inerrancy behind.

How about turning away from hate and retaliation?

There is a parable here
shot through with the geopolitics of ignorance:

in spite of an interior castle
we remain susceptible to so many viruses.

How about banning war in favor of meditation?

The Dancers

There are dancers in pink sheets of water
who cleave the leaves of air
they play the true flute
and crave the rib-root
· of the moon's dark daughter's heir.

There are dancers in jade lakes of midnight
who flow to sea with a sigh
where green goddesses walk
and forgetfulness clocks
and dark brides the light of the eye.

There are dancers in blue swans at moonrise
who wag the howls of a hill
and carve out the wind
on a blossom's red chin
until time erases the will.

There's a dancer in dead drums of summer
who hawks the blood-sifting ground
as bone turns the stone
of the everlasting foam
of the one who dances unbound

P'uhonua, Kona Coast, Hawai'i

A place of refuge, a second chance,
where no blood may be shed, a space
sacred before King Kamehameha where royalty
possessed that spiritual power called mana.

If you outwait folly you might just live,
understand how often a sacred burial
ground is beneath so many steps.

Imagine this planet as a gate of refuge
from total war, a second chance, where
no blood anymore may be shed,
where non-violence toward all living
beings is the law of our breathing.
Might we all then be priests
absolving one another for our
daily injustices, our blinding inhumanities?

After Surgery

My head reels woozy.
　　Humanity's music blurs
aglow with the miracle
　　of reappearing. All the anesthetics,
the robust inattention, and time's amnesia
　　cannot mask
the unmastery of pain.
　　That colossus always returns
to pillage graves and unmarked passages
　　and begins revising a poem
or the drama of someone novel.

This bodiless fact stands erect:
　　a part of my body's
body is done. A part of my history
　　is history. Sometimes we're
defined by the who who remains behind.

　　Pain I find
always takes me
　　back, enlivens me too
in a way, and never ceases

to remind me
what unbearables its attracts
        to be at all alive.

cloud-wisped afternoon sky
a wild gander skimming waves
takes flight

Feeding Pelicans, Sonoma Coast

Vibrations first, the air stirs
with six and thirty wings. Circling, they
angle again and loop, converging to
make a point.

            Diving, their
Z-shaped necks angling, from
the waves they fallen rise.
Fishtails in their beaks flapping,
their sacks stretching the time
for the blood of ancient sacrifice.

            Poised,
they swoop again with jet-back
wings, scooping beaks, horizons
rising, the catch speared aloft
from the tear and wear
in this one spot
the tides gathering do not
mark or wait for.

And just like that the frenzy's
finished. That craving, from wingbone
to the heart's darksome muscle,
bearing them borne again
newly south.

Reading Shakespeare's Dark Lady

Backtracking the centuries I
glimpse you Will cutting
through a twilit bush closing in on your dark
lady, that Moorish attraction lying between the acts
as distractions do. Your play, a foreplay
of words contours her odors,
details delicately her wired hair
for in nothing is she like the sun.
In your dun passion's suck
you don't seem to care
if her lips be coral—or where.
Your heart's iambs breathe
by the accents of embrace. You and all her
Egypt, as you take it all off this evening,
seize the summits,
as grunts shake those valleys up, your lines
making up hers, lies that in truth lie
in truth, those flatterings
your ink uses and loses
not.

Night Sweats

Your touch explodes
me. How can I forget bluebells
in bloom, those
cups swollen, and no less the
sweet summer grass?

A pulse this fragile, this volcanic,
takes the tyranny of dust
by the throat.

The Psalmist Thrums the Harp

After each blow her enemies smile.
They laugh over serious bluffs of poker,
A scripted score of power plays. At times,
When convenient, they display their hearts:
Lies to themselves in the concerted games of politics;
Lies to threatening others in the timbre of their fallen securities;
Lies to God glorious in the fame of their hypocrisies.
Clubs of jealousy, masterstrokes of the petty,
Footnotes to the banal, diamonds of envy.
A cunning refined by harping that awaits another hand.

Along Sonoma Coast

From the cliffs
you can see beer-white foam
sunstagger and fan the beach
wearing rock shoulders.

A harbor seal
lazily floats then dives between
swells and sways of brown ropes
of kelp.

From the beach
you cannot always see the seal
hunt. She blends in, sometimes
on her back, floating.

Listening close
sounds her sound: rap rap rip
for the meat inside, a mortal
circle, she cracks a mussel shell.

Sequoia

There were survivors in your family
Too. Before the kingdoms of Benin and
Ashoka's India, you survived it
All: denying spirit to matter, and
The healing power of rage, captive limbs .
Who freed each root's journey, those mother tongues
Of mutual emptiness. Other limbs
Became the heirs of worms. Through fires your lungs
Yet breathed. Circles of seeds became your skins,
Scars of your history, wood of our myth.
You survived as Lao Tzu died praising yin,
The Black Death cinched the dead, genocide blitzed
Us with ash. But before you're axed to jade
Your shorn limbs will hold more than this time's shade.

blue jays filled with sunlight
silent now
the peace of lilies

Rivers of the Sea

I watch the ducks and the fishermen too
And the woman who threads by the water.
A dog's tied to the rail of the trailer
She bought way back when her clothes were brand new.
Somehow she survives though not like who's who
In a rich loneliness but through hangers
Loaded with skirts and pants and choice strangers
Along the way. Beer, bread, potatoes, stew—
These bones help firm her blood. The fishermen
Too wait at low tide, their poles pointed straight
Down the river's 3/4 time. They chat low
In pink sails of the wind as a gull tends
The reeds. And the ducks? They mate and await
Greener currents, sometimes yes, sometimes no.

Symbolic Straw

In war as in sex
winter comes on dark.

Take that man floating
silent
as though dead
on currents which scarcely move
the moving river.
Birds hunger in limbs overhead;
nervously they watch him.
They keep waiting
for a thumb to twitch or a nerve
to unnerve.

So far, all they know
is eating
as a form of war.

Turbulence

Your bottle gleams half-
full as our captain comes on
and tells us what we are
already experiencing
this time over the badlands of New Mexico.

Through the window
mountain wrinkles are still half-
revealed by mirages.
Those are your favorites, *mi alma*,
something we can agree on.

My favorites are white cloud
puffs that hang suspended like gunshot
and spread their shadows over

a bluff's shoulder.
Still there are winds at cross purposes here
no matter
why the flight
or destiny of origin.
Tension makes flight memorable
you observe in this mating
as another mirage is spotted.

We cannot and do not elude the stress
but accent our way
through a canyon of clouds
as we steady ourselves
for the foregone
perception of a flight
filled at the last to half-empty.

Butterfly Dreams

Dreams of radiant lessons
wear your silence.

Their flutes map those blue eyes.
So you win in losing and win
through the trees of silence.

Such dreams skim across
soft years like ivory mountains,
blackberry refrains that secrete joy of a kind.
Butterflies light in the navels of clocks. They alight in
bearded roots upon mountains that stir
songs of the saints, songs upheld in the features
of stone minotaurs.

Though made at home, your vanishing cheek
is still startled to find lines stretched at 2 a.m.
by orange fountains that have that living look.

Islands of Indifference
(a picture postcard)
> *Lasciate ogni speranza,*
> *voi ch' entrate.* —Dante

Here words have their edges sanded
smooth so they mesh
with their opposites without effort.
Good and evil run as rivers of uncaring.
Hedonism—lush, tropical, naïve—is
their only god.

Their bodies lie
on beaches like sex objects,
garbage picked clean by
loveless buzzards.
And still is there the desire,
that native conatus, to pass on
forever in the sand.

Easy for them to whisper love
in moments and mean
nothing.

Landscapes here ape mere hunks
of well-hung meat
not as one might be, but mere
chemical convenience, gargoyles
in the flesh, surveyed by the latest
art of the state's technology.

Easy it is to defeat them;
their arms bend like willows.

Some never feel below the surface.
They abort on the tongue's premeditation.
Others finally reach their "other Eden."

Here they grow wings
and take another chance
to sharpen their teeth
on one another.

Evening Star

You brighten the red setting sea, break down
Toxins, those ice hearts, spider-
clockworms, myth
Shorn skeletons of unmeaning, unsound
Moons with robot hands,
                              rootless kin and kith.

No plastic fragments, you and I, but more
Than mechanical specimens, or mere
Tools, but hallowed with a human core,
Children alive, willows dancing the earth.

Let's relive the dream of that reverend
Future, where fog-lovers find starry nights,
And whole worlds pulsing alive know no end,
When imagination passes organic heights.

Venus can you, alone, torch up this rust
Lest our outcast parts mushroom into dust?

A Sheep's Remains at Fort Ross

The surprise of it could not be
forgotten: balls of wool still attached
to the leg joints and rib cage
which looked as though
it had been crushed at one end.

Buzzards and hawks had picked
those bones into a gray stare.

The wind, constant, relentless
as the steady sea roar a hundred
or so meters away, dried the cage,
ravished its decaying scent and
hollowed out even the skeletal neck.
Sprouting between each rib
and beneath sockets
where eyes once gazed
were tiny yellow flowers
on this headland so windy
only grass and miniature ferns
hugged the earth as close.

Degrees of Green at Goat Rock

from here you can watch
waves blaze into

horizons that bleed and stretch
to the sun's mediaeval eye

refining the sleeves of God

where waves whomp
screaming and sunshiver
in a syntax so deafening

they pirouette
in the moment of God dancing

Tulip Tree, Late Winter

The lady leads me to these pink bulbs and cherishes spring
unfolding in her voice.

She leads me through the seasons as though they were a history
of prayer.

"Love lifts the world." Day by day, whether sleeping or
waking, she points to each bulb, waiting.

(The hungry always manage to find scraps.) She leads
me to this unpretentious wood:
Get rid of all that is unnecessary. Let the story never end
the story to re-envision your home.

Match on Water

In fact we are lovers. You can tell
by that delicate fidelity
lining the eyes. How we hate
when staying moments go
but remain
captured and captivated
by last gasps
of the stealing sun
coloring through layered clouds
thin as venetian blinds.

Awe and silence
hallow this setting.
We pull warmth around us
like a circle, a sacrament
of touch, of fragile space
unbroken
by that jagged brow of breakers
come to gnaw the world.

And too our eyes are bridgeable
shores of the soul's country,
our hearts rising serenely
into the body's heat, its
passion's philosophy,
its awakened aftertaste.

And the sun? In seconds
it folds into gold and
with a final swoon, slips
slowly   slowly
into a bare squint
brightening, o brightening
at the last rites
and bursts into a match on water.

just when

1.

the Absolute lures my brain
and beckons

old Kant
(within the limits of reason alone)

draws his sword…
i become
categorically ensnared!

2.

just when
the answer to a koan
moves me
to push aside
a mountain…

like a Zen master
Basho deals
haiku
to the jaw…
exquisite—
nazunas in bloom!

Composition

We get masked by the lines sometimes
like a bluish dye. in the shape
of a wolf's rib. shot through frost
or that other tigress, fire,
and leave a licking trace
in the foaming measures of afterglow.

Yet at the center of this
where soliloquies intersect
and thread on, the unmasked abode,
where we're finally dead and being born.
This is what weds us
long after returning to the basics
of color, to fashioning newer flutes
for the longest descent, and to the
philosophic season
with its hammered truths, trans-
parent deaths, and beauty's
shoulders of corduroy.

The Millennium

Some gather at the river
Or dance to the gong

And bells, awaiting the feast.
Some look over this planet

And discern what is still
The pulse of green.

Others have a chance to erect
An island of undying trees and stars.

Still others rediscover the
Ancestral wound

And explore the continents of fault.
A wishbone rises to the surface:

In one direction, indictment for
The voices of terror. In another, a lineage

Of chance for the chords of dialogue. I say
Bring on the reverend mysteries, flavors

Of the magnificent.
Few mysteries have we escaped—

The sun rises, ever rises from the sea.

Winter Sutra

In each lotus there's a disclosive return.
In each passion an artist on the run.
Peer closely: between flushes of
Unearthy light the holy root quakes.
Birds startle at the moon's path.
Outer skins no longer hawk hunters' aims.
From lakes of vinegar paradise rises.
Beads like these entwine with mystery—
In its unbearable scorching velocity, its
Hearing through the sway of merely eyes,
Its threshold of the frozen—
The mystery that compasses us.

Veins

That leaf is
worth your study on a star-pocked
night beneath
limbs
whose veins shoot
through unscaled sight.
Through them

you summon up your lives
floating through to a summer's deep.

Some, bathed in outer dusk, crisscross
skies
as though surnames perforated
in blood, a milky talc,
puff of nothing.

Each branches
to make a past, crossing
over in a present that unfolds
vibrations of blue.

Cheekin' It

let's go, let's cheek it
and just go

leave it and fly
as wild geese fly

with our jeans on
(we've been penned too long)

grab your seas
by the wheel
the sun through
your mind
and let's cheek it

past pink clouds
of New Mexico
and beneath
the southern palm

let's go, let's outa here
and just go

no waiting around
to pay the bills

hanging around
to rent the day

let's swim through sands
past the farthest star
and catch a zebra
by the twilight wrist

let's just cheek it
and eat wild berries on
olde summer roads

and ski dark
winter swans down
till the stars
swallow the moon
let's cheek it

drop it all and go!

and sail the next wave
bravely leaping seawind
and soulward into spring

let's cheek it and leave
the worries
the dyings
at home in a jar

and scout
beneath a star's hymn
arteries of fire
as we revel in praise
the sun's sacred rise

Amenities

Her needles move now by instinct.
Memory's threads over memoried tread.
A patchwork between what is
In the cards
And secondhand gossip
Like the olden days
She still beholds.
Yet whenever her needles pause
As though suspended
There's a curious lethean air.

She remembers how it was
Some years ago out watering
The easter lily and the ash
When she partly unraveled.
Her eyes they dimmed
Only to disclose
A face strangely
Gentled. She remains
In yesterday's mold.

Her children have dropped by since.
And both times, no
Just once, they fought
Over the price of selling her
True estate.
Still she holds to the golden days.
A kind of peace with bygone griefs.

Her fingers are now moved
Not by whether
It rains or clouds, but
By instinct and that alone
Along those threads that thin.

The Stuff of Legends

One brush stroke
and mountains ring.

Waters tumble throughout the spring.

No longer obsessed
with pressing thumbs on the moon's
deflection or
spears cracking
this oh-so-nuggeted earth
or even with
three or more
in this misplaced zoo
contending.

But with one woman, a tender mouth,
an unforgettable heart. And home
becomes a door covered with flowers
that do not stay.

Seeing Deer, Jack London's Ranch

Winding slowly down Sonoma Mountain
splaying a languishing sun's
languid fingers into scattershot, past
curving Manzanita and thumb-
spired pine, we stopped in a twilight
meadow, flush with ferns, odors
luxuriantly lush with day before
yesterday's rain. Without warning
or brush of wind
their eyes
with sunsets blushed
rose

to meet ours
a deer grazing
with her faun.

Her stare grew bold-blooded
quizzical
frozen
between flee and flee,

cold as tough mounted
on darkened knotty pine
yet blown alive
with the earth's blooming.
We stopped
as when time leaves
breath bone-shorn then
stung on a stall of stares.

Protective, caution-reloaded,
exploring to the milked second
a distant intent, she waited.
Without moving.

Our whispers, whispered slow,
and endearing as any hart's love,
did not perturb
or wrinkle
as though she had picked up
the scent
of what
this open secret meant.
Her eyes lowered
for no harm's teeth pared the air,
no tang of death
razored close.

And finally flicked her tail

as we followed
those footfalls of ours
unbuttoning down the wild.

returning home from war
he walks across the sand
footprints in blood

moonlight on mountain slopes
strands of stillness
seas in motion

Creative Pulse

There are holes in the expected.
Repetition can leak. Long El Greco
arms reach through everyday sleeves.

You are not the serpent of someone
else. You are a black mountain rising
from the blonder hills. A creative
break from the biased mass.

Like uncharted lips you
can shape into lasting
ecstasy this novel
wisdom when o so many delay in chains
and drip slowly over stones.

At the Perfume and Makeup Counter
*Lines are described...by the continued
motion of points...—Isaac Newton, Opticks*

1.

Lines form wishes around these mirrors.

2.

Giggling girls vie for accents that linger.
They pour *L'Eau de Mortalité* between
Their palms to reproduce a timeline for feeling.

3.

Once he trims his beard, the former clown
Prefers to be made-up. He does not mind rose water
So he can clown around without false nails.

4.

A housewife pries her mid-life out of escrow
And, reading between the rhythmic
Lines, tries to relive the luster.

5.

An older woman, well-dreamed
With bluish hints to her hair
Rubs her wrists together to sample some *Youth Dew.*

6.

The pretty woman applies blush before
A hexagram-shaped mirror, pauses, then notices
How in the *I Ching* some lines are moving.
She senses how reversal draws the aims of destiny.

7.

They can turn mirrors by a wish of the wrist.

8.

Most try *Opium* at least once.
Or splash on *Eternity*. Usually there are
Lines brooding about the eyes.

9.

What counts is the drawing back,
The embrace, wrinkle-deep or not,
Of wear, an obsession
Whose age simply survives.

Seaside Haiku

out of a fog bank
skeins of hungry pelicans
scan swells of the sea

Keepers

for Jim Herrman

Finally dawn. Just above freezing. Now's the moment
to wake up. My friend says now's always
the time to try.

After much grumbling, finally I find myself
waking up. Already he has some
coffee on. And soon, still sleepy,
we make our way
out of this dark wood.

Day dazzles. Lake jazzes. No clouds.
From a high tree-clocked bank
we angle in and follow them—
rainbows. By the dozens.
He casts in. In seconds

a strike. He's reeling
now. Breakfast before
breakfast.

I cast out. In minutes
another strike. I'm reeling
now. But this one's no keeper.

At length we begin to realize
our seasoned limits.

Tonight as flames hiss beneath another last log
we too feel released
as from sleep
to grasp this brief wilderness
this paradise of uncommon air.

The Chinese Chest of Carved Soapstone

It sits in a corner, an enclave of childhood
memories, this heirloom
with a company of three riding a sampan.

The jaded one guides it into a feudal
river's snake-shaped mouth
on a riddle of emerald.

With black mustache, another rides
each fathom
tethered to cream-colored buddhas.

A third one aims his dark
homing bow
and shoots at time's galloping dust.

They dwell in one wonder, a kingdom
that vanished from the middle

which still bubbles with war's oldest blood,
sometimes drowns in a dragon's desire.

Amid odors of teakwood
these fingers rub memories of stone
with a childlike touch who laments
that wonder ever leaves.

Setting

Why? Need we ask? In quiet spokes of the setting
· eye, the iris, cervix once bluish with prints of a sun
rising from laps of dawn, like a dull shroud
envelopes your facial narrative, a valley where
your breathing barely sways mooring ropes,
intensive care in lines sketched with charcoal
and prepares this journey, a mere hair's turn
through an aperture of skull. And then stillness.

You are gone. Done.
And from our eyes humanity flows.

Your cousin Marie thinks you are fodder for worms.
But I recall how you once
came back, came back to tell us
of that spectrum, rainbow of your fashioned ribs
a glide through dawns
that sear so vast a sleep
when the only shooting is light, where a spray of a
thousand stars
radiates from the sun's throat, heartbeat
of mountains closer
to dawn.

my friend fishing
a sunrise pause
scales flash through water

The Queen Disrobing

Higher than this piano or that castle
overlooking the Bavarian Alps
your loves were missed in mist
like a train not taken to Kyoto or St. Petersburg.
Side by side we conducted
ourselves so that sky filled with laughter
and mopped up summer's thunder.
We felt mated with amazement.
Beaudelaire's uneasy spleen
could still play and draw out our best. But
After intermission we skated as sun to moon.
Respect's ashen hags tilted, flew away in protest.

All we held in common reverted to each alone.

Beaudelaire even dressed as satan's boy
you despairing states of his mistress, I
admiring his infernal flute, that
classic of the city. Now you pouted
and sat on opposites sides of the room.
Glowerings, pawings, and whinings
made us finally converts
to the estrangement of choice.

Shells

A couple keeps the pretty ones.
Homely ones they leave
behind for dunes of another time.
They do not seem to care
if cracked or chipped shells
yield their own summits,
pouring through this summer of driftwood.

Pretty ones, too, need a place to end.
Perhaps a book case.

Or part of a child's display, for
a philosophy tugs behind every period.

Yet even here still they can hear
the lonely armor
ragged scalloped emptiness, a voice that intones
blustery across the rock-scrawled sand.

Past Life of An Evening Star

Some days she can remember
The holy encores, stars she once
Played, flashes of cameras,
Her name pulsing the marquee.

She was everyone's envy.

Her name posed on lips
From San Francisco to Casablanca.
Now she stars alone.

A nurse brings applesauce, juice, and milk.
Old romances flicker while
Flirtations impress the flesh
With leading men,
Days when fame with champagne flowed.
The nurse guides a spoon
As a replay spans the room.
She asks who that beauty is.
The nurse upholds a mirror:
An occasion for fading recognition.

Reruns return the turning world.
Back then it did not occur to her
Which was more alive.

A Slice of Papaya

Breezes brisk as the spray of whales as flippers, tails beneath
the surface of the Kohala Coast, we
sense vastness in the way our legs cross, clouds whose roots
descend to continents of coral. We remember

Between lip and lips, this portion
births in small churches, the backyard under
flood waters,
a drought worthy of rain dances
bridges washed away between shipwrecks
and the scraping of forks
among the plantations, the stumps
where divorces graze, jazz resolutions
as violins play on tortoise shells,
golden tongues now silent
from this cold sun, these.

Most of all, this wedding, flames of our eyes,
dream horses
mutual respect, biographies
that stem from the captain
of our hearts.
Already leeward breezes, coastal sands,
hot to live in the spout spray of humpbacks,
dorsals of dolphins,
making memories out of more than sand.

Vermont Suite

Vermont greens
Deeper than redorange
Notes. Deeper still the boiling
Post-glacial springs
Where pools murmur
Vibrant with fugues.

Wintry tree limbs
Contain the psalms of summer
And frost hounds
Despite steeples sunlit.

Soon sleepy sugar maples
Yawn with an unhurried pitch.
Surrounded by dandelions,
A sorrel barn harmonizes
In May's pastoral beds.
Bridges timbred in stained wood pose
Accompanied by congregations of yellow.

Conversations turn in pink
Awe among levitation purples.
When rainbows round
To ultraviolet
Where what blooms
Stretches unspoken grace.

Six Poems

Cumuli gather like summer swans
As philosophers ache for what is gone.

*

You undress blue flowers at dawn
And celebrate the times in time's taut skin.

*

Cathedrals teach in the roar of glass
To breakers that whine for an hour's nectar.

*

You reach within for courage and color
And touch a seascape of hereafter's hand.

*

This reception weds two summits as one
To flirtations of sky, summers of dark.

*

With its zesty blood, your secret itch
Turns smaller hands into a stammered kiss.

A Book Burning
(Berlin 1933)

Midnight and thousands of students by torch light
decide to shrink their atlases, dismember language,
and engender their own
index to what the state culturally approves.
The plot revolves around the difference between
an old protest against the "decadent" arts,
and a new inquisition for thought reform,
a perennial appeal to those who want to feel
empowered or who have recently seized power.

Volumes of Helen Keller, Upton Sinclair, Margaret Sanger,
Freud's *Civilization and Its Discontents,*
with its analysis of aggression's
capacity to destroy civilization and
Jack London's prophetic *Iron Heel,*
go the way of Einstein's theory of relativity.

To hear their spines crack in the flames
(and here at least twenty thousand)
augurs a subplot and pretext for a final solution
where differences can be cremated.

Jazz out of the Blues

for Carl and Marge

faces in a sea
  wine-slipped
saxophones propped
  in vino
the veritas of art
  aging with mirrors
a jazz
  crystal image
in the tenor of sax its
  tenderest unfolding
hearing the source of hearing
  godawful diamond

  there's a collage of pillows
and chips
  eaten by inscrutable emotions

just the blues getting jazzed out of the blue
  pure joy the galloping
rhinos of daylight

archipelagoes that slowly quiver
  pouring out sundowns
howl after howl

  caught in wineskins
found in the paradings

Notes of A Survivor

How difficult to deny
The predator appetites
Especially during those searching
Flashes of light that erupt between the pines.

We have a rule: don't eat during the day.
After catching a glimpse
Of those cravings on shore we've found
We lose some of our best numbers
That way. Sunset's at both ends of the scale
For these authorities on a disappearing art.
Take my aunt: she went for it.
Poosh! Strung out. And two of my cousins,

They couldn't wait for the dark.
They resisted being
Obscure, without a truer game. Instead,
They leaped for the inviting lights, grave

Appeals of ear and eye, the sensuous razing
Of time. So far, I've strayed past the sign once
To the middle with schools of the others,
Floating counter in clockwise circles

Not to touch the earth or whirl silt
At the bottom or linger
Any longer than it takes to leap
Into the air, a wishbone of faith

And defiance. That way, I've survived
In this farm as one trout who can smell
Leaps ahead and trust the pool
Will not be cast further up.

The Decision

One may add wrinkles to any lover,
Settle for crumbs from a minimalist past,
Find refuge in a splintered flute,
And revel in our reductions to ash.

One can venture more than ethical bleeding

Or contrappostos that tempt a nuclear itch.
Or one can peer through postmodern pity
To undo unbelief with summer's fist.

Voyages
1.

Beneath a plastic defiance of gravity
In a jungle of coins and electric impulses
Through usury of city gutters
Passing around ghosts, tearing out hair
And the faces that cannot stop even
As summer slaves to death's wintry rage
In hawkish times when generations
Are still born to yank apart
And crack to forget
That one can actually live
Since speed is not all we are.

2.

There, in stillness, the timeless begins
Sacred, and, after many crossings, found:
Time for the birds of return.
Time for the revolution of wilderness.
Time for the wisdom of community.
Time for summers impassioned.
Time for breath richly-birthed.

It is time, it is time
To cultivate you and me
To farm the scale of vowels
Consonant with no-words.
Whose thundering silence
Gallops up a newer mountain.

Shapeshiftings

There is something that does not die, the destiny
of experience. God sometimes disappears.
The world's night is not always holy.

In fact we can at least be double-minded:
the lucretian prelude that may ripen into Don Giovanni,
pilot molecules on a slope of slippery
calculation with gas enough to liquidate the
human and reload the pelagian guns.

Or where waves née particles prefer
(and cometh now, love, the mystery)
in dancing solitude the beloved
community, intricate logics of soul,
butterflies angle in resurrection's motion,
and the unwritten destiny, your original face
before you were born, first insights invite.

You Remember Windermere?

And loves on Ambleside green
As gulls through iron-blue wind
In their pretended alliance with fish
Angled only to eat the turquoise silence.

You also embraced Lake Ullswater in your blue coat
And red hat while tracking legends and novels
In highland breezes forgetful and flowing
In an August sun that seemed to stock the angelic
Behind the loins of afternoon and confessed kingdoms
Beneath still-life skies of your gentle
Surviving bones kissed by islands histories.
Summers there touched and buoyed your muse
You found yourself in clouds and clover
In fields of sheep and grassy solitude—

Such were your summer's parting waters.
You remember Lake Windermere?

Telegraph Avenue, Berkeley

Pizza from Blondie's by the slice with
pepperoni curled to the bourgeois edge.
    Books and more books redefine
lists of which bodies to read.

Cries of pasta, delectable proletarian hash. Incense
    Wafts down and over boulevards of beads.

Celtic crosses. Lip earrings bespeak the mother tongue.
    A revolutionary spirit smolders in the alleys.

Harrowings of hell gush from the record store Rasputin's.

Aaron and his arm-in-serape mate, Jamaica, wear
banana republic caps that spell "Trash the police."

Meat rots, nosedives, smokes up funereal—
unless to protest a squad car cruising the People's Park.

Earrings in her ears mark protests about to ignite
pizzicato arias in the wilderness of Godhead.

Here flyers resemble sermons that fall limp with
civil disobedience within the *anima mundi.*
Jazz, blues, and perfume seduces where the mind
    stretches over the unearthly heritage of introspection.

Chords in D major flow nowhere, modulate,
and return to a war of causes.

For Those Far and Near
                              for Lani and Barry
For some whose love loves deepest
End far from those best beloved.
Long fences, miles by silent miles,
Far begins when near should be.

By kisses, word, or parted lips
Leis of aloha or touch of art
Miles assume mirrors that linger.
How exile returns as love delights.

Second Reading

You can wake up, earth, and do not have to
Commit history without thinking. Or release
Memories emaciated by barbarism.
Or convert to daily doses of dictatorship.

Always there is room
In the dictionary of angels
Where you can unearth tribal thrums of your
Natural caring.
Deepen ochre prayers of a brooding pleasure.
Recover remedies that do not harvest
Terrorist seas,
And dive headlong into the lotus of breathing.

Drifting

No direction. Not afraid to wander.
Beneath a relentless sun, that lust

by lust, feeds on a dreamless inverness
of scalloped ice, I reclaim myself.

Not for anyone or a tailwind's sponsor
or for love hereafter.

Having nothing, I celebrate the
fever of saxophones and run before the wind.

Grasping at nothing, I allow to flow over me
the current's unseen irises of seduction.

The Snowing Art

Horizons of white silence.
A march of seduction.
A new wave of white on white:
Snow falling as though unfallen.

But art layers by contrast
The human tracks
That will not likely restore such waves
No matter how jaded or purple
The footprints, how
Burgundy and mandarin those telling desires
How grayish that innocence.

Nevada Beach

Here seagulls spread smells
of a timeworn fish.

Around that elbow of earth
a dog romps in the olive grass

as though bitten by her inheritance.
Twilight, a mist teeming, appears as a guest voice.

Drifting with certainty, a pelican
swoops, reeks a famished philosophy.

Aroused, nearby fish do not shadow a given
line. They fly for the unwitnessed deep.

Somewhere, just above the vanishing point,
lurks the bloom apocalypse.

A Shadow's Tale

What hell to be mere reflections
Of the other's will,
To exist through another's arms,
Assume day's the only wife
And see our nights foreclose
Into mourning bones.

That's when we live invented silence,
Suspend trust,
And dwell in forgetfulness
Of our time's first face.
We end bequeathed to an era,
A tree dead with promise
And take comfort in ravishing weeds.

Poppies Gathering

Green sloped searching hills
   splash toward the sea
with its dissolving beaches
   and cormorants diving.

   In mustard fields, out of
darker spaces, these tongues
   exhale sunlit
flame orange to breezes
   swaying wild in manias of joy.

   Beneath theologies

blue shadows interlace the journey—
behold: this lingering fruit
the lovers almost.

Lazarus

Lazarus was worth a laugh
In snow-shaved winters where
Alone in far echoing woods he could recite
Souvenir verses and poetic snatches
From brisk evening airs.

Arias of summer came and went.
Lazarus would play in bales of hay
And listen to his radio.
Not once did he seem to mind playing
the joker at our banquets.

Autumns rolled like water falls
Whispers of age almost forgave him.
He was no Dionysus.
Yes, he was old.
Mountains seemed to grow
At his feet.

He *was* crazy; at least that's
what we *thought*.

Scenes from a Reality

Fingers around this pink
rattle, a majesty of gentle blessings,
grateful roots.

*

The mind and its events

survive peninsulas of praise,
unfold and grow as seabirds
glide farther out to sea.

*

As if shooting outward,
nebulae flee
to follow those dark
stallions of the sun.

*

A scarlet Macaw and keel-billed Toucan
rest in their rainbow freedoms
drawn from a mythic continent
over a generation rising
to chart a novel latitude.

*

In their virgin bowls
Buddhist monks find Mary
holding fast to the Tao
as it weaves through testaments
of being and non-being.

*

More than edges separate kings.
In the kingdom of the fall
flesh floods the years
with pantheons of
borrowed illusions.
Despite this, queens
still urge their sweet prayers.

*

Fingers around grateful blessings,
aprils of pink rattles,
return to those gentle roots.

Dangling

At the mercy of the wood warp
Of indecision, between the famine
Within and a compass without range,
I still dance in a sea penciled with despair
For I have learned to float
By not always trying to fly
With every dandelion self that lies.

In this field of tenderness
Like some classic gesture, I catch the moon
At its crossing and wait
For a tide steeped with the naming
Of ecstasy.

White Clouds Off Sausalito

Fix your eyes on that breast
of earth rising in us
noted above the seaboard smell
and hold them like apocalypse's
breath that magnifies. Soon
a mast begins to jut
its solo transmigration and segues
home from whatever war it was.

Gulls know the measure of this symphonic
gesture. They hardly blink when light perches
above shirred swells swollen black, or
as now, when the mind's timbre
glides pulsing seaward and seeds her
doings that urge and billow

tender as pregnant earth,
gracefilled even in snapping canvas
that knifes the graying tides of tympanic skies.

Deeply, breathe deeply, for these swells enshroud
a woman's bowsprit face, one that has no rest
without love, beneath prevailing winds   .
where many, many have loved her
under sails that billow half man, half woman.

Found In A Copy of Gray's Anatomy

Of course there comes a point
when illumination
appears as death
when fire's streak of forgetfulness
is almost expected.
Yet the grass grows
and buds break into midnight horses.

These impulses
(or maybe intuition)
of a widening vision recollected
urge the seer in us
to dare God without the veil
as when genius cleaves the temple.

As noted before, roses are what they are.
They cannot open butterflies of stone.
Listening to them listening
in the ripeness of summer
they rescue the range
where the silence sees.
You have already tasted
how close death
grips madness
and films the history of wisdom

even while standing in outlaw rain.
Just don't forget rainbows breathe
in the smell of hay.

Seagulls, 1944

Ranking with the oldest of trades
they were called seagulls. They served
the fleet to the end of hand-guided seas
when prows entered and sirens tugged
at Pearl and the Philippines.

Their charms encircled as snake charmers do
young seamen. Their liberty followed
liberty with another proposition, their bodies
sleek, bejewelled, hardened in sea-hatched
breezes where mates, in their ripening unwisdom,
netted in them a shoreless dark.
When they caught sail, they spread in port.

As the anchors raised, their hearts parted
even in the face of faceless memories, fading, as   they
sometimes do, like silent sunbursts in snow.

They returned when the ships returned
to leave unfathomed
that circle of meat lovers bound as the tide.

Midpoint Bridge

Beneath a sun that is dying
Barges plod lazily along the Seine River.
Twilights strummed softly at a guitar's distance
Become the clock's primary food.

A woman in blue flashes
Her eyes, smiles from the heat of initiation.

Three cats, including an orange one, purr
Next to yellow flowers growing out of a red pot.
They relax in the wintry prayers of September.

His emptiness unused, a fisherman surveys
The purple streets that pose no answers.
He lives to find textures of joy
In a cloud of tones.

Two Stones in One Sun

what would we do
sans fire's stream
and water's sand?

no sun makes snow run
no silence swallows sound
no man yields woman
no god finds human ground.

suns and moons
resign their turrets of jade…

it finally takes
a you and a me
to fell the bifocal tree
and dip blue guitars
in the earthiest of moons.

Seeing the Blind to the Weight Room

"Try these on for size," said the one who peered
through his shades, not wanting to be seen.
The dumbbells rested until the blind one curled
them away from gravity's angle:

up

down

up

down

with every labored inch, muscled
into delicacies of forearm and triceps.

"Okay, I dare you to try those," the shaded one
said, trying to weigh the outcome. The blinded
one positioned her hands with a light touch.

up

up

up

all the way

up

until she nudged the stars

The seeing one's unbelief grew heavier than his
shades: he took them off to inspect closer:
he could not believe his eyes as he measured
what nonsensical exercises she could see through.

More's Resort

Another sailboat glides down to the bay
in an everlasting sun
that tempts the ancient color of lovers
and records the unbreaking of desire.

Inside, beneath the slow-motion fan
this joint speaks: the computer game,
Conquest, a virtual unreality, blinks beneath
the Olympia Brewing Company poster.

Another wrinkle urges: Red Wolf Ale:
follow your instincts.

On the far wall a framed photo of San Francisco's
Cliff House with smoke curling
through the windows during the 1906 earthquake.

Early afternoon the jukebox belts out "Ramblin' Rose"
and how many pitchers of beer later closes
with "The Fire and The Rose."

This one's the second to last resort. Here Horace's *Epodes*
assume an intimate texture
and take on a home page all their own.

> **pine needles whine**
> a boat rests on water—
> three ducks feed

Perennials

Roses my friend offers
drip a slow pace.
For you, she says, *a bounty.*

Fragrances of these confederates
light up
for me marines of the dead
where stamens sustain Shiloh
and memory's crosses that endure
stunning white in Flanders' greenest fields.

Outside Auschwitz lilies
mark the blur
of biographies, shoah, indelible red poppies, cinders.

A thin dust floats

blooms stretch skin above Hiroshima,
eyes, wake by swollen wake, sealed.

In 2020 as if from purgatory in 1945
A mother and daughter await
a father's return
from another zealotry bound for North America.

Flowerings suspended by centuries
march in a riot of shells.
Black swans encircle, in baby's breath, continents
that divorce, marriages that outlast
the last.

From the earth, they're for you,
she says,
perennials.

Atlases

We discover each flat globe
inflates, assumes the direction of none.

You press and press until your nail's
half-moon horizon
snows into a sea of brown.

(that's *imperialismo* for you)

Along the Zambesi, Africa searches
through the debris of geopolitics.

My grasp outmuscles the Arctic summer
as Asia rises dripping with
prehistoric jade.

(there's no limit to continental rift)

With herculean difficulty, your veins
voice the pillow of our brevities
where ticking seas once roamed.

Maybe as early as the absence
of jailed lenses
we may rejoin once again
the uncaged heart.

Sea Swells

The sea battering
a rock before sunset.

This close to dangerous rock
consider how fierce the momentary becomes:
seasonal riptides and tempests resound.
Safe to be strong in sane moments, a peace
that recalls the flattery of posterity.

But the pregnant wild that turns tomorrow into literature
bonfires, lights up cormorants
that assume black crosses, deepens the deafening
erosion that is the small price of survival.

Here too is ecstasy, a peace
that is no imagined life
but swells the shells where serpents coil green and gold
hiss gold and green, green and gold.

waves thunder waves
pelican swoops
a fish tail goes under

The Saying

What is not
said or lined
between the covers—
the flurries of form
through sutures of thighs,
seas tidepooled in mountains,
nuclei that sway blue-hot raindrops,
praise beyond
a mission of similes—
these are the saying-nots, talented
blanks that
discern invisible planets,
blow out of glass
an angel,
craft out of the holy,
galaxies.

For Simplicity's Sake

Throw out those theories of mind,
Anguished wrestlings with dandelions,
Pennies dreamt by the nightmare's pull,
Those howls of paperweights.

We are simple in our complexities:
No-mind *is*
a laughing matter.

Not to Let Go

I have seen them
Throw a pathology net:
The mothers who live to possess
And fathers who gamble to neglect
Trying to relive ungodly bones now dead.

I have watched the love that smothers
An individual perception
With rules that blind
Love that confines
And sterilizes the body's mind.

To possess is to kill
All love that is will.
It will kill joys as they fly
And shatter whatever tomorrows
You could weave into song.

She

This desk, the ebony one, white with heat. How I know it.
Scribblings by lamplight
circles, blustery nouns, arrows, dishwater adjectives
all cross-fertilized and recrossed.

Long into the nights she would write. These curtains
swayed with each breeze. Summers and cicadas
came and disappeared over the hill.

Her words the broken eyelids she adorned, those pulled out
tongues from chaos, were the symbolic moves
forged by the collapse of distance between us.

We are getting to know each other, she would say,
pursing her lips.

For her, each passion was a cloudtree
from our ancestors who watch us
while we sleep. And hers thumbprinted a
mask with words in blood.

Happy the silent listener, she would say,
pensive, downing a Black Russian,
who hides from us the fever-inclusive past.

Sometimes in snow I can still hear her
leather boots crunching choppy ice-fugues
· where the unimaginable aimed to reckon the dusted
ambits of her soul.

Even then we could winter with a winter's mind
and find resolve in a
concave mirror, a moon's rise for each lingering bird.

Fishing Spanish Flat, Lake Berryessa

Here we the contented just could be educated.
Cans of worms only stretch so far.
Wind swishes through that window's silent definition.

We listen to Dvorak and Ellington, re-read
Borges, and Basho. And novels thicker
Than ceramic plates.

The afternoon opens an olde disclosure
Of wars and genocide; castles in ruins. No black love
In white walls. Abbeys and empty beer cans ping
With sounds of quail shot.

Though being eaten—entropy for the masses?—
We long for the force of art, the spiritual that does not snap.
That is what future biographers may not understand.

In Socrates' Long Shadow

Religiously you offer no answers
   easily plucked.

You question and waver
   for your daimon is a turning,
a refined
   blood giving of thanks,
a subtle revolution.

   Those shovels turn on logic
and tune in
   to reveal an ecstatic
earth, rivers that rush
   upon indwelling time,
ice plants that poke and pull
   through the dunes.

Parting Song

We come as one
to where rivers diverge,
remembering the clear light
is the shortest inch to the divine.

And bearing ith astonished lust
a more natural light
where egrets come to drink
impermanence
from each new address.

So we go, swaying to stars
and thickets of journeys
larger than us
who only wanted,
in the thinnest membrane of home,

that heart-fonder state
lips to lips alone.

When Music Dreams

Through dreaming seems
Awake to be—
Apples compose your dream.

In times of forget
Listen to remember—
Wild surf in true November.

Seeming grows
To perpetual stills—
Lupines realign the hills.

Dreams dream to remember
Who forget notes that scheme—
Learn to be, yes be, in the fiesta of seem.

Forget will's forgetting fare
Seems remembers ages—
Hibiscus for your hair.

Grow to wake
Play to seem—
Only petals dare scale the dream.

To Kiss the Earth Again

Untie that mind
reasoned to death
above thighs of the earth's last moon.

Clear the debris
of intimate scalpels
and live the music unconquered.

Untie that body
and let ardor rip
tangs of the smoking sun.

Meditation at Sea Ranch

Each tangled passage, gleaned or mottled through
Contains a translucent realization:
The haunting hinges of waves crawling curved sand
Or young grass laid bare, a new sunmaiden
Bent by a tree-jesting wind, hawks with
A wing for blood aim with an aim of bread,
Cliffs sea-drenched, raptured, steeped in sun-lashed myth,
Brush yellowed, browned by rubs of late summer.

Finally, *mi alma*, the one pined for,
Bewitching, curvaceous, deeper than nights,
A kind deathless face, steamy, alluring
Lover, hankering flame, ignite into
Deafening silence this aroused screaming sea,
When my wet body slips into your sun.

Sawing Wood

In uncut wood one way yields
To cut, a message you can deny.

Another angle or degree to avoid the field
You are and flow with all that be may be?

Should a saw's teeth crook and warp
Your true love molders.

Against the grain, best blades dull
To revel no more.
What intimate finishes you are cry out
Though many saws saw louder than love does.

Perfection

Certainly for perfect certainty:
The logic of a clear light
Or the nude of beauty.
Not the logic of rebel angels
For the settings of all suns set.
Do you dare a perfection that does not
Relax in the pauses or
Where doves repose in the pupils of tempests?
Or wager a perfection that suffers
Beyond the visible
Without the usual tremors of the world's wild mouth?

Then, in a ripening expanse
The nobility of surprise
Raises a mirror up to that restlessness
And finds you in your secret imperfection
With your vulnerable certainties
And a blood that takes on the aura of "shipwrecked."

Revisiting the Demonic
(for Ray Bradbury)

> *By the pricking of our thumbs,*
> *Something wicked this way comes...*
> —Macbeth

In a dry crackling autumn
we rediscover the fiend
mingling in every man's masque.

We have to look twice;
our hearts cannot conceive
that smirk of attuned cunning.

We had bet on shaman's visions
but they do not heal deeper than myth.

Dancing clowns remain aware
a joker warps the deck
of alphabetized desire.

When that carnival train comes to town
its last station is the lure
of empires, galaxies with no apparent end.

In its cars lurks an antique edition:
the eldest fraud, unmasked, thawed,
diced breasts dangling from infernal lips,
its human glowing wired to murder features.

We had squandered reservoirs of divinity
until our latest lights had to reface
what seemed once only fictive
and stomach once again how wishful illusions blind.

What We Do

I chase after robins and valley quail
into the tulips of afternoon.

You dodge relationships that lure
questions from theological meadows.

I embrace the cheekbones of wisdom won,
insomnia's garden without all the blanks.

You explore the wolf without illusions
and start fires that master nothing.

I tune pianos carved from hunger, footpaths
to that island full of ducks and willows.

You navigate the tides of sleep dancing
with pallbearers in the company of eden.

We angle for a halo of snakes and breathe
for awhile a peopled solitude.

We allow fences for fears, paeans of love's
nothing, and embrace the unwrinkled kiss.

No. 3 Gun Turret, USS Arizona
(sunk at Pearl Harbor, December 7, 1941)

Feeding gently they glide among shadows
And over copper coins tossed by well-wishers
Who cannot fathom the tides
History wakes
As though coins can do more than commemorate.

These are not reef fish
Like yellowy Convict Tangs with black long stripes.
No, these are Sergeant-Majors
Complete with bars and stripes that rank
Among the living.
Below tourist decks they swim
Where the curious lean
Reeling in their reflections
Through prisons of air.

Around guns that circled once
For the state they feed
Casually, unaware of how oil embalms
And still seeps to air

Or how marine life engraves skinless
Fingers to delay corrosion
Of the memories peace amends.

Shadows

> *Chacun est l'ombre de tous.*
> —Paul Éluard

1.

With you to kill one man is to kill all time's
flesh-sawn waste.

Contemplate that scarred moss-slicked
moonburst evening within

itching to chant *o dark film darkening
become that lightning voice where mountains free the heart.*

2.

With you to compose is to sketch
the first course of the first citizens of chaos
who return, though the deliberate eyelids of
fable, to the returning art.

Pray you, teacher of oblivion, rip open your blood-drawn
blouse and caress the flanks of dawn.

The Lovers

Their profiles suggest robust
latitudes in marble, lip by lip.
Nakedness unhurried,
the bronze of repose.
But you, in the old
mercuries of joy
and grief, and I

through ticking biases
carve us
into passages
a genesis, constant
the cunning,
blemished
ends of beauty.

Medea

The man you made
has left your bed.

For a younger woman.

And more power.

You might say
an upward career move.

But your moves
are laced
with a darker craft.

All from a bitter half.

And what of your children?

A custody battle
or maybe
the premature labor
of an unfit grave.

If your Jason only knew
what bloodletting
it takes
to make a break
past burning fits.

Quarries

I am not a predicate.
My quarry is spirit manifest
as nature and history.

"Among the covers
of any dreamer there is
a euphonious shell,
replete with history,
that does not pine.
Along with burdened lizards and trees
it still points to the joy-stocked
shelves of silence."

I tell you I am not the subject either.
But a nonlinear quarry in between.

Triumph of the Will

Then came thought control
In the name of a new world order

Of robots, technocratic reformers
Who did not mind a return

To a time before amino acids.
Nuclear fallout was urged by the will,

A cult of unthinking, clones of fear
Reared their heads as though their true gift was dread.

We became a cult of collective suicide,
Purveyors of genocide, the silencer of choice.

Since by itself the will is blind,
Insanity gradually became glorified.

Since we believed thought was too cerebral,
We goose-stepped our way into being true believers,

Surrendered our reason, our intelligence to mass man,
And annihilated the planet.

Now that liquidation is nearly complete, and we lay dying
In our last hours, this consolation is ours:

At least ours was the true politics, the right religion.

Cutting

for C.P. Cavafy

cardboard boxes
in the garage with a coral blade
the fluent sun a mandrake
melting me
to turn again to Colchis:

thinking of you Cavafy
on your meanderings to Ithaca
or
poised for releasing
love outside that blowzy cafe
awaiting the spitfire sheets
of Eros
your clothes half-torn
in the grotesque
glare of day
where you embrace
a passion distilled
a politics that remains
unwearied by the Greek sun
unwithered by the Byzantine sky

Dental Visit

Hear that tongue move.
Against the tooth, inside this cheek.
Along these prehistoric molars.

Hissing the air it gives birth:
A little world
Conceived in sound to sound out this one.

A pause between changing saddles
And the vision of God.

Between the country and the city
Roots whisper something
About human fate, dive into time's curved space.

They taste how the tongue glides
When the silence, in a breathless wave,
Still has this much to say.

Beside the Petaluma River

Touching this wind as flies bend the weeds
I lie here next to brown logs where boats tie up.

They come to shore as the sun empties itself
of any companions except one.

Tomorrow is supposed to explode in storm
across a plain of crosses.

Green is supposed to burst from
the loosening earth.

No gloom and no grief for those
who celebrate the rain.

Or for those who behold solitude
past the scent of the naked mind.

Homing

I celebrate you
God like the innocents

the beauty
of lovers.

So many winters
have I flung my sad nets to the sea
and lost
even the scent of your name.

Rain

We surrendered
through our cravings, embraced

furies in those philosophic limbs.
Our days somersaulted in the wind

bonding with the invisible.
There were wrinkling horizons, way back

then weighty in the April solitude.
And salmon-colored sunsets,

grave with a future's dreams.
Nights dancing through each lotus-kiss.

A kingdom that unwound, long in passion's teeth,
summoned again in the earned wisdom of rain.

The Black Ducks at Pacific Grove, 1956

They live
 in the tamed expanse
 of a white country

standing
 on briny rocks whitewashed
 by looms of the brood
 wings poised to impassion
 as though
 waiting
 for their time
 when white no longer means
 the absence of color

readying
 so they can soar
 past graves that have no ears
 and roots in unsung bones
 rather than mill about

watching
 pelicans fish the surface
 seals turn to rock
 and those periodic gatherings
 of lonely hunters

Doctor No

     Occam's razor de-
constructs the common
thumb, announces coming monsters,
moons with bloody spots,
a turtle on its back in late winter's vowels.

Not

to mention lusts of willows, players
spicy with allusions, a genesis
that does not
end with amens
declaiming in unriddled stone.

Who breeds a future of none:
no context
including interstellar histories

no insights
beneath current power plays

no horizons
deeper than paper wounds

no flesh-hewn
psalms uttered truth like that.

Moonstruck

[based on partially imagined letters between
the author's parents]

Driscoll Hall
School of Mines
Socorro, New Mexico
March 3, 1933

Dearest DeLores,

To answer your question, that's why I'm here.
It's a chance to ride out the Depression.
I've seen bread lines snaking their way
In each town and city coming out west.
Yes, I agree, engineering may not be
As tantalizing as my darker love,
Poetry, but you know how succulent it

Is, how that bewitching siren bewitches.
Poetry so disrupts, ripples silk sheets, it
Glowers dispraise at last. I suppose each
Of us early or later has to choose
Between the fondest heart stealth or the head's
Cubed room, between triangles within and
That depressing elegy of what sure
Pays. A fact that lives: quantitative
Analysis coughs up more rewards. So do
Casting and alloys. But I must admit
Sailing those waters with you summer last
Past Portsmouth my peace was unalloyed.
To you alone my poetic cast still flows.

All that is, is for now. I wish you could
See the way clouds pink here to purple peaks.

Goodnight my moonlight madonna.

Dreaming again,
moi

Old Hickory Lake

Shoreline cadenzas hosted
A café of whispers.

Odors of magnolia
Encircled luminous fireflies.

Lake shadows massaged
A sleeping turtle's throat.

Our marshmallows caught fire
In the blood.

Little did we fathom
In those last kisses

How August suns are
Loves gone under the hill.

Starving Godward

Shadows of nothing yet we,
though loveless, press
the irrepressible glass
and watch the sun's arms radiate
dying to rip the dark.

Time cannot resurrect this watch
but only recounts the fight. It is we
who eclipse the spark, fish past
the way.

Boredom's where we dwell
and ensnared by despair's
latest leaves of sense
we can become unraveled
in this love
quest. Amid this all
we still can recall
the way
dark shades home.

Glass fractures but can mend
when vision enfleshes
and ends end. It traces us
with a joyful wisdom:
a graced release, islands
recast, fathoms reborn.

That elusive vision, mystical, *vita
nuova,* rejoices in the catch.
How it yields in the reluctant yielding
cornets of praise, homewards of bloom.

Between

the fury and the serene and still
a marriage that's actually
marriageable
not as sedate as
the dead still living

nor a passion
devouring the last souvenirs
of what makes us
us

but a yard
in between

where we go and plant
the feel of love
the invisible's lost kingdom

and
where I leave
to meet your planes on arriving

this cherishes us high
as irreplaceable
and allows us
to bottom low
as almost forgettable
should the unrisen arise

this is where what can be

can be on even ground
against all the undated
odds

They

through the trees they come
to gun you right through the riddles

they come at dawn
and demand
your proper credentials
to molest you
beneath towers of skulls
from sanity committees
that specialize in disappearance

they heap you
by medical experiments
and conversions through incantations
of terror, rape and hard labor

few fathom this dehumanized earth
where laughter and military forks
empty gold fillings
to mint a killer language

plotting the master plot
out of the foreigner you
the daring swallow in you
their target for bayonet practice

filtering out that passionate blood
that dares protest crimes
against your humanity
with beheading contests
by recruits in their sexual salt

setting innocents on fire and license
to raid rain forests to coin
a new kind of fur

where every thin membrane of civilization
odors the jungled

at a nail's width you could be
crucified and gunned
in crematoria of sky
one blade blown at the knees

when they terrorize
and demand you become they

Sweet Milk—a System of Signs

A woman dressed in treble clefs
dreams of love
becomes a gate for angels in designer genes.

She translates the sign
"Blue at the bottom of the pool"
and smiles as though armed with a smudge of suns.

She muses how everything certain
is hidden
in the swishes of a solitary falcon's wings.

Still she dreams, sings to the moon
dancing in the lake.

Her song points to a tranquil night's passage,
a swing of beauty's sign
restored to an icon called time.

Translation
(near Santa Fe, New Mexico)

Love is yours to translate
From the tolling vernacular rung.
Lips, tooth and tongue and all
That meaning means cannot say.

Here in the range of the Sangre de Cristos
You find love in a higher tongue
And need a ladder no longer
Than the one called silence.

Shoes and Glasses
(after hearing a broadcast claiming the Holocaust never happened)

1) Shoes

Black ones wait here
For a train that may never return.
And over here some yellow ones,
Red ones, white ones, some heeled-well.
Over there with their toes
Left up, some flesh tones peel. They're
Bulldozed, stacked high. Some actually
Have their soles intact. Others, you can tell,
Were at one time resoled. Still other have
Their tongues removed.

Even the tongueless can report
Mass murder as a final solution to flesh
That descends daily from each cattle car.

2) Glasses

Some spectacles leave nothing
For the visionless to spare. Others
Do not grasp the unspeakable.
This pair has the lenses crushed,
The rims bent. And that pair, inclined toward the
Archetypal, intimates no final resting place
For the ears and eyes.
   (defiance will do that)

There is a slow sense of hurry here
In this spectacle of inhumanity
To escape or perhaps foil
The reich's truer blondes, those traffickers in genocide,
 Famous for the fatherland's technical efficiency,
Their ovens mass-equipped
For the exile of us exiles.

There is, as well, a sense of staged calm
That masks hysteria
As these infants and mothers and uncles
And daughters and aunts and sons and fathers
And cousins and grandmothers undress and
Clench a lump of soap colored flesh
As they leave all supposedly to take a shower.

The Winners

for Max Money

No way to win this one, I thought, no way
Since these jocks leaped hurdles faster than I
Had ever done. One's time, 14.5
Seconds, set a record in recorded race
Before I even started. Two stars, they
Brayed how fast they'd go and lose us behind,
Said they'd cheer us from start to finished line.

Into the blocks we set, arms taut, legs spaced,
Spikes shot like smoking tires, comets that shred
Space. At the fourth hurdle both stars crashed and
A third was caught.
                        We took ribbons, hardly won,
But finished our personal lot instead
And found a way to see in such a span
And fashion some stars from what might have been.

Canoeing

The way she breathes with each deep stroke that feeds
Eddies and swirls, her paddle arches wide
As though to turn. But the currents that breed
The most difficulty are those well-tried,
Need deeper strokes. They're biases that shift
Their histories along the waterline
With scars. She finds it hard now not to drift,
To keep stroking in despair's wake, to find
Cathedrals in waves, genius in turning
Back to where she's come from, sometimes has to
Steer toward the shore, avoid the current's
Mainstream whose sunset cargoes can slice through
Some that are unsung. She knows too how pools
With each stroke change, how currents vie like schools.

The Port of San Francisco

A windy, clear day
in the soul of the body's wartime gray.

Blown clear of fog,
there spreads a mercy
so unreal
peace and parades
sweeten the hour
of each unbelieving year.

Last Leaves Last

Each autumn I collect fallen leaves
And file them away
In leaves of a book.

After years of keeping within
Their meaning's leaves,
I opened the book one day
And in swirls of dust
They all flew away.

I knew Eden would come again
This way.

Virginal

Then, too, April ebbs
on that unmated dock.

Once the dock rested higher
so little below was visible.

Now I follow the darker light
into shadows of shad, mud flats with granite faces,
broken rudders inclined to drift,
through angles of yesterday trees, mossy,
filmy, slippery as the time of beats.

Yet this vista, a survey of dreams, quivers
with widening currents like virgin terrain.

I am venturing to another station and sense
starry beginnings between the usual cargoes of grief,

a time and times swelling
to meet the plane overhead.

The Seals at Fort Ross

Waves plunge and plummet and clash
Over them as they lounge and shift on rocks below
These cliffs adorned with crustacean-gnawed hieroglyphs.
They do not mind
Withstanding the salt-wined muscles of the deep.
Somehow they sense desire
Does not run out of time
But parries and thrusts
With the tongue
· Beyond the fiercest breath to decipher.
Not only that.
They accept the surprise of daily thanks,
The grateful drama of reunion
With the salt of their own blood.

Love's Body
for Rita

A bearer of peace
your mountains
ever so graced
with mists and dancing leaves;

All the playful clouds
                    of you
are peace in me,
and in your fingertips
            God finds a way;

Ah, love, let us run
on sun bright sands

and embrace in summer spray,
shape ebony castles
and delight in suns
between our toes

and drink in
                a mystic communion,
love's body.

Your arms awaiting now
the peace I am
              with you.

A Circle of One

It flows where apples ripen.
Along the way rocks
Dissolve mirrors of snow.
It becomes a true cast

Of black spaces, dominions
That wake to lost friends,
Goodness betrayed over tomatoes.

It delights in tide pools
Where starfish stick,
Holds the hearse's wake
In a forever called the sea.
It caresses close unwashed
Silences, love does,
And tracks the
Center of the sun
In the furniture of each dark music.

Watching Whales

Brightness invades by wind
and waters as they dance
in this land, sea, and sky poem.
      An apple orchard's scent
tangos while the sun drowns.

Each isle in the current
weds us to the sea's swaying emotion,
          propels an epoch intent
that roars through the heart.
          Closer yet
the massive mouth with
          songs that suggest the hunger
of their compassion,
          faith in plunging water
that bumps, fish dives, swings
          down those kindred backs,
at a depth mortal with brooding,
          older in the joy of their songs
sonorous with adventurous breath
          as though asking how we come,
how we come to realize
          that all who breathe
may dwell poetically.

Two Addresses

A crack in the earth? Then regard yourself as
          fractured. Nature consumes you
with an austere silence.

Your body's field: freedom in promise.
          Greener than river-sky—
those subtle editions of carnations.
                    *
And you now: freedom joyous in excess.
          Regard yourself as a moon no longer
caught in branches, a lesser simile of the sun.

You are celebrated in a joyous
          dance; thereafter caravans
the sure courage of why—
          horses unveiling transcendence.

Match on Water

In fact we are lovers. You can tell
by that delicate fidelity
lining the eyes. How we hate
when staying moments go
but remain
captured and captivated
by last gasps
of the stealing sun
coloring through layered clouds
thin as venetian blinds.

Awe and silence
hallow this setting.
We pull warmth around us
like a circle, a sacrament
of touch, of fragile space
unbroken
by that jagged brow of breakers
come to gnaw the world.

And our eyes too are bridgeable
shores of the soul's country,
our hearts rising serenely
into the body's heat, its
passion's philosophy,
its awakened aftertaste.

And the sun? In seconds
it folds into gold and
with a final swoon, slips
slowly   slowly
into a bare squint
brightening, o brightening
at the last rites
and bursts into a match on water.

City Spent

Worn out by the dictatorships
of pollution, the perennial promotion of the less
worthy, the restless addictions
of noise, the parades of victims
in the square, rumbles by gangs
of revisionists, the routine
beheading of vision and idea
and the daily dung of official lies...

Worn out by all these
I go down
to a field
called Miwok
where the middle ages
breathe vigor
into the magnetic futures
of history.

At daybreak
a lake full of ducks
shines there.
I hear the tinkling
of sheep grazing
from out of the still

life of their inward eyes,
and cows, attuned to
the universe,
chewing away
the salty
haunts of afternoon.

Here twilights cradle
their unsigned and
unplanned grace.

Out of this silence
these words resound:
all shall find today
in every cubic riot
of prayer, in that
harmony that was
before the
elements were.

This clearing
with its conducting layers
is where I begin
and where
with resolution,
clothed in the dancing alchemy
of the sky's eastern wind,
I once again resume
where words dissolve
and become a virtuoso
from enclave to morning star
and one, finally one
wilderness with all that is.

The Point of No Return

To arise at once from the dead
Is not to be tied to a ghost,
Not to be literally read,
But by magic fly past the host.

To not be frozen in the lost,
Not to be literally bled,
But by magic free past the ghost,
Is to rise here now from the dead.

starlings

convolutions, double helixes
          swarms in dark clouds they
fan out amoeba and rifle-
          shaped, photonic
pulsings that march to time with a hundred tulips
          swarming
thickets of black sunlight
          cartwheels of foam
blue horses of snow they
cleave and leave
          smokecurls of locusts
cheekbones inclining, finger
          flights, hairless footfalls of air these
black bandits swoop
          and saddle
into self-generating
          jelly clouds, worming
and storming scores
          of night
word-boats, hammering
          undulations of black necklaces...

The Day After
for Rita

Sunshafts flicker through a caravan
of cumuli.

Steady surf whomps and hisses
against the rocks
          where mute armies of seabirds rest.

Looking up, spume-blasts shoot
through the skyline—
          a brief wilderness of snow.

As you sleep, I entertain this new relation,
a rebirth in mid-sentence,
                    two in the incomparable
company of one.

You encircle me:
family-veins rooted all the way
                    through the invisible.

Today near the river's mouth
where sand itches
                    to meet the sea
we remember only yesterday
this wedding.

I'll cherish the sun-veins and delectable
joy in your looks long after
                    my bones are mountains
and salt sweetens the sea.

Existenz

Not the whole day. Not even the whole slice.
But a flare, a sunrise, however
damp. One filling of the lungs, in love's
bruised wake, and you can rise
to eat the sun.

That is what is missed
when edges are pressed out past
the urinary gold frame;
a larger understanding
can prompt you
to miss the blues
in the hands of Renoir's
woman at the piano
so you do not live your heart's summer.

Brokenness is essential,
the shorn limb that maketh whole.

Weathering

Roots arm deep
and do not
buckle in a chaos of mind.

They abide and persist
too deep
for what ignites.

The sea washes in and
fire draws its character
in the sand.
There's a courageous
rhythm in presence,
erosion without erosion,
a setting sun that endures.

And all the while
you beside me
in this wilderness
always discerning it seems
centuries in forgettable stone
and seas that long
for the river's mouth.

Breaking the surface

Voices of summer
stroke by stroke
break the surface

Gregorio in The Garden

Wearing his yellow hat
and tan jacket
he does not even see me
in the window. Nor does he seem
to notice the snake
curled by the fence

whose chary black eye
coyly follows
his opposing moves.

My neighbor likes his work
as he kneels pulling weeds
from this love garden
so it does not have to be
mowed if it rains in May.
She likes the angle he uses
to cover all possible grounds
under pink and pale orange
blossoms by the concrete birdbath.

Gregorio says the secret
is to pull weeds
at a divining angle,
to make clearings
even on rainy days.

With his money he will buy
some time to dream
of the contours of the Guatemala
he once knew
and the woman
who still grows in his love.

To the Highest Bidder

What can I do in Rome?
I never learned how to lie.
—Juvenal

Cameras and advice-riddled heads
tugging at your abuses of power.
Images, paparazzi, confirmation questions,
Hostages, arrogance and hush-money.

How easily the difficult path seems,
how the original signature can disappear
or reappear only to succumb
to sex, stunts, and symbolism,
bottomless sleaze and scandal.

Avalanches of questions
surface for the original designer
befitting every taped discovery,
the most difficult
the odyssey of plotting your own
divorces through whatever turns your
circles take, through visions
that tunnel among the sirens
who can make you sing in tabloids
those sticky time-warps called betrayal.

The Liberation of Eve

Eve Caressing The Serpent
[sculpture, Reims Cathedral, France]

Nor your stony legs and and arms tremble
at the snake's insolent cry
(or could it be a last laugh?)
its tongue centered in full relief,
its parted ears frozen
in thirteenth century gothic.

Does the snake become harder
to bear through stitching time?

Do you envy its deadly aim?
the design divinely used
to penetrate your paradise
foaming in the fall,
leaving hope alone?

In your chiseled rite
do you peer into Mary's unwitting face
and wish you were God's end?
Her heavenward trend?

Or do you see yourself
dancing carefree, anonymously
through dusty mediaeval fairs
with those money changers
beside their fish stalls
at Milano, Magdeburg, Beauvais?

Or playing Death in a preconceived gambit?

Instead, you are your own
apple tree-splitting tapestry
to leave undone,
coupled with your own
hardened snake hardened
to caress forever
in a judgment of stone.

2. *Breakthrough*
[reflections on sculpture, Reims Cathedral, France]

Finally
it dawned on us
you were not a prisoner of stone,

120

that you had other choices,
and Mary's virtues sometimes
became a vice
grip around our vision.

Now
you and Mary go dancing,
Adam plays the alto sax,
and you are friendly
with all the girls.

Now
as then Jesus comes
and changes
water into wine;
for him, everyday's a wedding:
he would never
cast you in stone.

Eve
your beginning's end is just
another means
as is your winking serpent.

You can lay
your burden down
and swing
above this garden of earthy delights
with God now dancing
out of stone.

Apple Dreams

Apple dreams bloom, seashells that cradle
roar at the losses.

Eyes buried long ago, you've lost

at love before (as have I)
between firesides earth and seaside sky
you sigh, you sigh dare we try
again
although there's summer hays to get lost in
and hide such longings from midsummer
roses, safe, unfound.

But hiding is to die
and not string violins in bone.

Love's best again and poetic—
can *we* roll back the stone?

Apple dreams bloom, seashells that cradle
roar at the unknown.

Tea and Biscuits

As we talk I am no longer with you
Though tea and biscuits touch my lips
And talk runs through endless sand;
We are in moments one, mystical,
Apples in horizontal arrangement.

Being there, we are not,
For the listener hears nothing call
While the eye draws its inward tongue
But gets entangled with that lesser one,
Talk of "you" and "me."

Still. Still. We are called
To compass a divinity sunslant,
That distracts us from these biscuits
As they brown, having cooled
In that state, like us.

Weeds and Snakes

Clusters of weeds, like snakes
On their bellies, perforate
The plastic grounds cover.
Weeds the least reputable; the
Snake equally tempting.
We, in grave accents of loneliness, are
Relieved to find a familiar face, a family
Branching that sheds and disposes skins of ancient bias.
It is like meeting an old man in a garden
Who resembles the one you once badgered
And who now strikes you as so new.

Crossing the Oldest River

This shore rots we thought:
Bodies tanned with unbelief.
Music taped over the unending
Crack of desire.
There were deadly odors too.
Chicken livers rancid with easy griefs.
And eyes bloated
With politics as usual.
We dared to long
For the other shore
Where a little red boat
Docked and swayed,
Where summers of love
Collected like rosaries.

After passing the unimaginable,
We reached that other shore
Where tomb-quilted quiet surrendered
Bliss without clockwork,
Where the unconscious
In full sentence found itself

The unsigned
Source of a more cunning blood.

From this noted kingdom
Punctured with tiny drops of ennui,
We began to look back
Along our novel animal tracks
And long through mists
For the aboriginal shore.

In those browning bodies
There was dignity,
Strength made mettle
Through enduring grief,
Arteries of joy
That penetrated even
Uneven suffering and
Courage that followed courage
In the fallen shoulders
Of our twilights.

That Taste of Nectar

Nectar on the breath? A quiet storm?
   Resurrection's seed?
Further down, the magic inside
   Where the measureless hibiscus breeds.

A breath? Such a reflective blank dives
   Deeper than seed itself
Down into the marrow of things
   Where doves, in moods of snow,
Rest on waters known as the "ancient truth."

This storm called the dream
   Is the mightiest dream, silent coitus,

Where words ignite like pampas grass
   Before the "eternal."

Again a seed rises, tastes of nectar,
   From the roots of runaway sky, and
Rises into a footing of clouds.
   There, lovers from valley pools
In a spirit deemed legendary
   Earn their genius in gulfs of dust,
The realms that move in God's dream.

Weaning

Some days he wanders
off and loses
traces of the who
he once was.
Tried by sheets tied
to the bed, he rises
like a jailed nightmare
ablaze through the elders
and goes.

At the park he resurfaces,
his fingers flung past desire,
and absorbs the terror
despite milky syllables
of the politically familiar.

He shakes as he enters
the outer dark, past
least visible lines
of persuasion until
the lights all dim
down to the inaudible,
his mood to the no longer

foreseeable, leaving
the hysterical
of who remains.

with the sun no longer

cold
the Buddha sat
beneath heaven's tree
and traded
one mortal day
for a diamond cutter

Gulls at Jenner

Where the Russian River
rejoins the sea

a way back from that sea
strand's spume-plashed rocks
with nosy harbor seals
a wind-quiet ritual
of land bunches them into
a surrealscape
where memory
caws just long enough to eat

where clay-blue time flattens
into the jaded cargo
of mere being

where listening dunes
shade a forked sun
that nestles ankle-deep
in the suddenness of sand

this lightens their sacred space

Rainbows

Unbutton these precedents, yellow,
and peel capsuled pastures
        where
blue liquid sky reaches no limit.

We voice suburbs of orange, reflections
        terraced deeper red.

Green's the innocence that forks
        in passing.

For all the Ducks I've Fed Before

they're always there, feasting,
stroking, pleading, sleeping
sometimes plump, usually quite round

almost too plump for mating

London, Nashville, Valley of the Moon
they're always there, eager
for bread on the waters cast

hens quacking, drakes colorful,
quieter, their orange feet lazily
trailing feathered entourage

primping, diving with wings flashing
or feeding poised with tails pointed
heavenward,

daring you, just daring you
to do something
about their brief exposures

February nights warming
their beaks beneath wings
in down and down

then April's rituals leave
breeding marks on the rear
of the hen's nearly drowned head

they're always there, feeding,
stroking, pleading, sleeping
sometimes plump, usually quite round

Necessary Guides

There is a guide to a life
where pleasure means more than fame.

It speaks of a voyage
through a country planted in many generations.

It is at times a seismic
return, that inner ear, prehistoric,
a sutra of secrets where
cherry blossoms are always about to fall.

Yet fame too has its lingering times.
Sometimes it is here,
at others it
scopes an alternate universe.

Sometimes it just devours
your own hands,
assumes a darkening ecstasy
and ignores
your cultivated ignorance.

Words from Life

Headlines can shock her.
Or, like cookie fortunes, they can amuse.
Ads at the back of the paper await
Like subway passengers classified
By their stations.

Death notices seem
To grant her one more release.
She scans the names, the loved ones,
And ages when their psalms of earth
Sang last.

Addressing birthday cards, she realizes
That, like firewood stacked
For the winter, they too
Are numbered.

While playing tarot cards,
She tries to pass over the death card unnumbered.
That way the deck remains alive.
Her cards soon cross that shapeless bridge
To what shapes
Words can ill afford to say.

The Drive to Order

That vase by your window reflects
the storm. When thunder pounds
and rattles the pane, the vase leans over,
as if drawn to the windy sheets of rain.
It does not lean too far but rights itself,
obeys the laws of physics and karma.
Outside, in the rainblown trees,
chance redirects limbs that bend and snap.

As you brood by the window, you realize how
landscape may reflect on mindscape.

Hawai'i, No Ka Oi
(Hawai'i's the best)

With no useless hands, the wind
breathes aloha through the palms,
splurges white caps,
bends masts and sails,
hugs valleys and cliffs deemed sacred,
bares truth, crushes illusions,
fields rainbows and taro roots,
sways chiefs reading the stars and
clears harbors of mists and surfers caught,
wrestles dragons with teeth of hot coals,
turns goddesses to dancing around ancient fires.

In tumbling snows of the sea
this fierce wind paddles clouds,
windburns lovers and fishermen,
and leaves corals and sand crabs
strewn on the beach.
In the rhythm of warrior-waves all told
this battering sea-tempest
crashes as emerald foam, blasts forms into new ones,
swirls life around then whomps older and old.

Learning to Ride

Make sure the girth is tight around the belly.
Hold the stirrup steady.
Put your foot in and swing up and over.
As desire shows, you may act like you have
Mounted a mountain. Hold tight the reins but none too
Tight. Don't let this behemoth swim away.
Stay on as long as those captain feelings allow.

The saddle may slip but hang on and
Into the waves glide away. There are times when
You may think you are drowning. But when resurfacing,
The life of breath, with all its talk of death smiles,
Celebrates as though it were the day after paradise

Stretches of Summer

Wind their way across these cheekbones and thighs.
Such raids make veteran branchings of smoothest flesh.

From the fall into summer's browning innocence winter
Seems to linger as any patched lineage does

As though these limbs hang heavy with unseen snow.
For now its aging truth has receded.

But its hidden wrinkles, those worn stretches we wear,
Turn into a destiny, a destiny remembered,

A half-seen life of life
When those seasoned interludes reflect us.

Pigeons Homing

Masters of return, their wings, dashing in flight
Above the tall eucalyptus trees, a display for hawks

On topmost branches swaying in sunslit gambols.
By the emerald fishpond, breezes pray and sigh

Through high-grown arches of graceful bamboo.
Santa Rosa plums purple deep in pensive August suns.

On the garage roof, almonds lie spread out
In cardboard boxes and continue to simmer.

This time the pigeons return from beauty.
They know home is where they're from.

Beneath the Art

Days fade like old words:
their poetry dissolves,
dirges unto death,
that borderless garnishor.

Days do resume, of course,
once words for once are reborn

and broadened again by being
reconnected to silence.

No longer does literalism exclude,
choke, and narrow those lines
poets, wordsmiths, and saints,
in their hushed roots, draw from.

Then words are again empowered to
slice through diamonds, ignite
distant forests, and cherish ecstasy,
the secret life of silence.

Today's history lesson

Today's history lesson:
Gold, greed, genocide:
We don't have to repeat it?

Devotees

Spring plows turns of earth crushed slowly beneath his moccasin feet, the moon half-showing, the scent of apple and mint cut the salt spray, the swells of sea almost quiet, break with a low murmur on the gravel-like sand. Wearing blue denims, she, curvaceous, black hair hung lightly over her shoulders like a shawl, wears spiked heels. Refinement is an order of her blood. In the twilight, he knows her voice, sound of the Sea of Cortez, when she calls his name. From behind a tree, he appears and waves: "Hola Nirvana." "My Aloha," she returns. The sea, in its tides and time, exudes saltiness. Between breezes, apple, mint crushed, newly-cut grasses seem a tourniquet. In the distance, a construction crew talking, at intervals joking like card players in a game of chance. In turn, she, listening to the sea, the workers, calls back "My prince of Maui." The scent of apple turns more acerbic. The steady throb of the sea lulls them, the sound of chimes rides the wind, the drone of workers, all orchestral as he calls "My dove, my black Madonna." She holds grapes aloft; he comes toward her, holds her in his arms, addressing her as his dance of the cosmos. Such lovers do not die in a vineyard; they fall into a light sleep beneath odors of apple and mint newly-shorn. Dawn breaks more yellow than the persimmon tints sunset usually reports. The construction crew drones again, scything their way through layers of rock and chaos. Still he wears moccasins and one earring; she spiked heels. Between kisses in this valley of lovers, this valley of the moon, they knew night would come again. She now whispers "You are my glad tidings," He kisses her hard. The workers drone on for hours. The wheels of lingering crush more mint. Apple dreams perfume the air. Finally she says "Farewell, Time," tenderly. He adjusts a string of cowrie shells around his neck. "In some parts of this world, these count," he says with a smile. They embrace once again. The breezes seem saltier now. "Goodnight my serpent, my beautiful question." They wave again as they disappear between the mountains and the sea. For a time, that scent of apples blunts the zone of construction.

standing with you

in the grammar of death
   where burning
mothers unending desire

where sanded cliffs
   vie to bluff
the solvent sea's resolve

where the mortar of centuries
   knees the dust
and then dissolves

as wild scrying dunes howl
   spume-spray groundless blows
past the masonry of island names

still the sea   the sea   the sea
   rises to read
the deepening moon

and with unerring
   unsteering intuition
pauses its ancient menacing

(and oddly at the address of death)

allows loves to follow love
   that utterly speaks from stones
and anchors unanchored time

A hot June day
cold beer
this temper dies down.

Between Snow and Memory

From the scales of illusion, this love survives.
The rains come, the grass grows.
Snows bury, memory stokes
The smoke of myth, the bird of tongues.

The rains float, green the grass.
From the scale of illusion, our love yearns
For tongues of smoke, the birds of myth.
Memories grow as snows flow.

This love learns, scales illusion.
As grass cloaks, the rain still shows.
Snows flow the way memory knows
The bird of myth, the smoke of tongues.

The grass it grows, the rain still soaks.
Our love burns this way, embraces illusion.
The tongue learns myth, the birds of smoke.
Memories roar, foams as snow flows.

This way love learns, shreds illusion.
The rain shades, grass dries.
As snows flow, memory roams
Past myths of birds, tongues of smoke.

The rains flood, the grass hosts.
Memory saves memories though
Myth's a bird, smoke has tongues.
From illusions scaled, this love survives.

Days You Died for Me

I should have known the day
roses came
anonymously. I

just thought it was a friendly
gesture. Not long after
you said you would not be seeing me
anymore.
That last night you denied and denied
even seeing them but finally
admitted
sleeping with them
all along.

In that last hug
on that last night
with goodbye blanketing our bones
in spite of promises
again on our lips, I felt like a
fish bellied up
to be cleaned
when the knife slowly slits up
the stomach from a point
behind the gills.

My eyes dropped out.

Sleepless nights and tempted
a hundred times to call you,
to feel your warmth once again, I realized
you were hard as rigor mortis.
Now in dreams
I watch your ashes in slow motion
stream endlessly
from an urn
from a plane flying low
and bouquet the tides with dust
that never will return
to the you
I once loved, once knew.

A Tyrannosaurus Rex Named Sue

Hollow bones of a carnivore,
elongated teeth that tear

jaws that crush
bird-like hips,
claws that rip the dead and the living, the holy
terror
of the flesh of creation, bubbled-up.
For millions of years-dominance
now dust
as though eternity wears only one design of skin.
Resurrect bones of the past and discern
a future's prints.

Could Sue smell a meteoric disaster
coming in the sky?

And what of us?

Will our own inhumanity, our own technology
mushroom us?
Or will we escape long enough to finally learn
to care enough?

In the Tao

Silent in the void
flows the Tao, a block
uncarved that yields
no desire, no marks.

Easy the way Tao flows
natural as the river of heaven,
effortless, spontaneous, ready
to reverse fields

in and out of emptiness.

Tao deeper than being
and non-being, so silent
the Tao and the river
are one
where breath blows free.
At peace before heaven and earth
Tao the name of wonder,
the sage who has no-name,
who lifts the sky by getting
out of the way.

Ladybug

Beneath
  wistful hedges
flowers
  wreathe
veins
  of your eyes
swell
  their beginnings
float
  under those soundings
your pulse
  arising sunwise
as the ladybug
  hops
from wrist
  to hand

Fort Ross, Early Autumn

Cattle in solitude graze in the burnt umbers of autumn
Where foam encircles boulders laced with sun-dried moss.

A brisk brine-mingled wind flavors this mediterranean of the sea
Cartwheeling over fomented rocks as seals sunbathe.

Fog engulfs the tops of pines in shadowed mists.
Eucalyptus leaves form beds on the forest floor.

A sea otter surfaces a melody's throw away
From a vigilant pelican riding the waves, driven by design.

An erosion-felled tree with its inbred limbs
Reaches toward the sea as though vying to find the first one.

The horizon blips silver, sun-skipped, gray
On darker gray begins with swells of kelp ropes.

One gull perched on a rock awash with each sea-splattering
Picks apart a glistening fish.

Out at sea, a whitish foam-lane, in plays of a lesser sun,
Streaks across that gray mass, brooding with seaweed sways.

The cove's sea line laps salt over lusts of sand
Where half-life shells beckon, sirens of an unfeigned fortissimo.

With force and voice these touching membranes
Play to shifting lights, murmur textures that color.

Skylights

Yours to try and keep, I take in all
I can: legs, pineapple, moans,
Coffee cake, slices of apple, massaged parts,
Yesterday's passions unbound.

I let loose the sun with a thousand diamonds
Into your history's prisms
Without words

Streams of the unconscious
Not even my light shows.

So you go and come again
And complain of the angles
These historic frames enlighten.

Soon you debark with those petite stories,
Fables to live by, recipes to go over,
While higher in this tree I remain
In souls more private than windows,
However clear, may sometimes reveal.

Fishing Carmel Beach

August white sand, a driftwood tree
wind-savaged against
blue swells,
three seals surface amid swarms of fish,
survey their feeding ground, discover
the coast is clear, cloudless.

Suddenly begins the chase,
slashing swells, fish flushed, fleeing
seals converging
to hierophanies of blood,
flippers pulling in the sea wind haunting, raving
aim for teeth-tearing, flesh swallowing, bubbles trace
swerving lines of silvery fright.

Then eight and ten pelicans in flight dip
into strains of memory,
swoop, listen for parallel tenors of flight, fish
for mercurial ripeness,
resume floating unfettered waters,
eyeing fins that disappear,
scaling down to scoop cold blooded heads.

Down the beach, a hush cresting
into November sunset
as three seals seal their gathering fates,
pelicans glut their horizons, seduce that craving.

Anniversaries

You cannot step twice into the same river —Heraclitus

Through this window the Russian River
reflects a shallow
smoothed out surface.
The same as last year.

And with its hush
a creamy moon
unfolds
into circles of yellow.
Much the same this time last year.

Headlights snake along the cliff-
riven coast past Jenner
then seaward to Salt Point.

We hold hands, fool around.
Seems the same as last year.

Yet we now behold newness
in sameness
when for a prolonged second
ritual's silent genius
enchants our novel eye.
speaks the speechless.

We unfold like the moon
whose shimmering
begins to echo
threads of blue syllables
intuitive cadences

of the awakening heart. Now
burns through the
undercurrents of seem. Definitely
not the same as last year.

Sunset, Kona Coast, Hawai'i

for Rita

To the south massive layers of clouds
form island mirages.
Below, lava rocks porous black
once liquid orange flame
vent Pele's volcanic dances, hissing
sulfur, ashen lunar tides,
withstand erupting turquoise surf,
dervishes of spindrift.

This setting's redorange yolk,
penciled with cloud-gray veins,
breaches that moment
when it rests lightly
on the sea
as though embracing for the first time.

We know work alone sets our suns,
snuffs out
explorations of rainbow solitudes,
eclipses the daring art.

Here we taste time
stopped, live beyond these bodies
in the way love frees, in new birds at dawn,
conversations of raindrops,
cups cracked,
plates with prints color-faded,
in the rhythmic rubbings of palm fronds.

The Homeless

In each city
With walls and without.

Cardboard dreams and plastic capes
to keep the stares buzzing off.
A park bench, a grove of heating pipes
there they dwell and steam shirts undone
the most public of our private selves.

City lights blink; they awaken
as pigeons feed. Blanket rolls harden
when the ground grounds colder than hearts.

They become amusements, freakish
carousels with cigar store Indians
for riders, for passengers who do
not want to explore personal biography
and have their veils of illusion rent.

But they are human, you and I,
us and us, different circumstances, altered hems,
exchangeable as native clothes, humans more
touching than words.

December's June

for Rita

Love is nothing
if not
thoughts of you
dripping hotter than summer.

You are love's habit
of bearing
the wintry sun
with burning ease
of stroking

143

my face at daybreak.

The unconquered earth
of you tempts me
to pulse on forever.

You are Mallarmé's sea breeze
gathering me
into quaffs of climbing bliss
gathering me
into sleeves of liquid desire.

To Savor

wine, slowly swallow. Savor breezes yellow
in shoulder-high mustard and in
fields where summers rise.

Savor the courage of one who outlasts
the sluggish times of average tyranny.

Savor each moon that rises blue
through the bodies of woodland pines.

Through the slow drip of winter
foretaste once again new wine feelings.

Know too there are rhythms that elope
and savor lilies filled with sunlight
in this streamlined waste of hurry and bury.

Eros at Fort Ross

(Czarist Russia's trading settlement on the northern
California coast [1812-41]; its last commandant,
Alexander Rotchev, was a writer, translator, poet)

we kiss on cove beach

the coolish sun smoked yellow

hovering above turquoise
  swells, their manes curling

the fog primeval, mists billowing
  landward engulfing

kisses (you are so warm my love
  I look up:
the fort basks, its redwood
  timeless, chapel orthodox

more kisses (you are so warmly loving with
  salty breezes bathing your face
fog enshrouding vanishes the fort

  magically the fog replaying
overtures of 1840:

  Aleuts hunt sea otter
Pomo tribe members collect wild berries

  Alexander Rotchev by candlelight
pens a poem about death...

still another kiss (i dare open my eyes
  gulls squeal, sheep graze
cliffs and fort dazzle
  now reappear

yet another (i love being here with You)
  warm, watching as seals bask

Lost and Found

what
is
found
in
lost

is
self
sorrow's
ground

but
found
sounds

the
lost
sound
of
found
the
next
journey
down
deep
down

Fine Lines

There, right there, put that finger in between
Tires worn and unborn threads: such lines melt down
Through the soot of innocence. Once so free,
The sex of history has tightly wound
Us. We don't feel deeply hate's loyalty,
Its gray intent, rank portents, savage mind,

146

And skies of snow? Or hear love's treachery
Illuminate the way trees pine and pine
Like fumes seething within volcanic rock?
Between time's left fist and the right's coiled wire
The body's clock suspends its tock and talk
When desire scents disdain beneath desire
And ice through fire senses *there's beauty to live*!
Living where the dead don't know they're alive.

Sailing

Sails skirt on glass
as the mind's timbre yields syncopation.

Easterly winds carry
the flesh into unmeasured scales.

Still pitch resumes
skilled at love's canvases and wakes

while the mind's textured reach
(without the shadows of jaws)

sails bluer waters that tint
deeper than mendicants do
with unconscious direction.

Miscarriage

Over your lips tears
began as the sound of waves
tried over and over
and around to form again
a picture of no one.

No one at home. Or maybe just
maybe hiding.

Suddenly lonely and stark
the womb still complete
with a walnut-sized
still life, a journey within one,
without a beat for two.
Sadness shredded those
corners of longing
with deadening silence.

All we could do was hold
on and bear the ticking
loss ever ticking
beneath roots that yellow,
a death as close as no one.

Existential Predicament

Our voices no longer tend to unison
In these boats drifting across dark waters,
No renaissance culls an older wisdom
From city lights or pain's empty daughter.
We are drawn from the earth, broken, skewered,
Shrunk to puppets, faceless, a mere maybe.
Here can we barely survive the sewers
Wave away newly-unearthed galaxies.

We can become these thrown, bitter fragments,
Pallbearers of earth mother's wartime zones,
Stars that shiver blue, breadlines of mass wants,
Rootless in this defoliated home,
Joys lost, souls unmoved by unmoored arts
When music's eclipsed by these graceless parts.

Canticle

We bike our way
along ancient streets and sun-shaded markets

with their fish, egg plant, tomatoes, purple onions and peppers
near souvlaki havens and snowdrifts with spleen,
throaty canyons above lakes of beatitudes,
past schools where children rehearse
the dance of future leaves in a mother's hair,
riding past formations of genius
next to sailboats moored in coves
amid the hairlines of anytime solitude.

We curve past men and women reading between their lines
as a grandfather balances a butterfly in his open palm.

Once through time-jagged mountains, we explore
valleys and hills where women gather clover for cattle and
where runners pace their way through decathlons with a drawl
while telescopes expand domains of discourse that expand us.

We glide our way
over underground cities and undersea villages
with their muffled rumbles
and listen to bards celebrate
unpicked passionflowers and skeletons of former days
for the being of time in time's art of the world.

These strains of the world that set our hearts on fire
snake their way through the wanderings of our breathing.

Healdsburg

Midpoint October. Layers of leaves
careen into summer's passage.
Last blazes shiver on
the Russian River.
Winds still purge as they did in July
and from the falls voices rise
sounding motion within the rock.

149

No one wants to go home. Not even
the fishermen and children
popping balloons.

On the bridge cars chase
reflections bouncing off waves.

Further down river, its whistle belting,
a freight with a cargo of timber
pauses to couple
awaiting the signal *heave*.

Oars dip silently
as two kayaks
slice through the bluegreen water.
Along a slope of sand
a dog breaks into a fresh run.
All the while
summer still tugs.

Confetti-light leaves shimmering
by the falls
reflect
the motionless eye
of a dozen blackbirds
peerless, autumnless,
resting like charcoal buttons
on a seasoned transmission line.

Late Summer, Russian River

Endless
   the desire
to halt the hum
   and buzz
and buzz
   of passage
and clutch

         what bubbles
from the restless heart.
    The blood
no longer curious
    flows
long into shadows
    to learn
a latitude of ripeness.
    Still
there is this yearning
    which juts
past the mellowed
    senses, past beauty,
to master fire,
    to season
the discerning eye
    for twilight.

Late summer survives
    when our
shadows engender praise
    at dusk.
Even now in this west wind
    with desire
pulsing with currents
    this yearning
is there, to climb
    down into
the root of stillness
    and touch
her holy skin.

Summer Hawk

Circling then drifting, black wings
tipped in gray, alone in unblemishing

blue, his eye scouts oaks below
that hug the Russian River.

Talons fleshly crimson, he circles
and glides, drifts, encircles,
searching for something, more
than hunger, a source of yearning,
measureless.

Maybe in bamboo banking the river
he will, among priestly shoots
and green turtle holes, unearth
his passion. Or in dreams coiled
as though to spring.

Cutting's Wharf

seagulls begin soaring
where a fisherman reels in,
a mast flag's skull and
crossbones ripple at anchor;

a second fisherman
dozes: his pole droops between
green hills, a hate-free foothill
of salt, and a *beer on tap* sign;

a man and a woman unload
on a swaying dock as
a white yacht's props
wake and curl the Napa River
without ceasing;

a scarf of geese
knit a *V* weaving the sky across;
an olde ship's algal-green hulk
and ribbed outline languish

into the ghostly unveilings of days:
in its sabbath shadows
grass shrimp tease shallow bass
as the between-rivers of silence
bends some deeper tules
while the sun warms the history
of gulls gliding and gliding

Russian River Ode

Your waters,
beauty stretched
with momentum
and etched from pain,
are a testament.
Along your oak-sashed
shores and among
daystar-brightening pines,
barbecues, campers, and wakes
of drifting canoes, there come
aging lovers
coming home to die
like whales beached,
eaten away, their
hearts exploding.
They are lovers
who by longing
lived, some
already dead
as they die,
love's rock bleeding
up their sleeves.

Loneliness in mortal circles
mushrooms
within the algebra of twilights

for they too long
to hear
your husky throat
searing with memories
whistling through willows
and boats moored
to a truceless sky.

They too
watch children
splash and kick
those huge inner tubes
and imagine themselves
tied to the balconies of heaven.

Yours is a testament
to their courage,
to hawks that circle
in this land of initiation,
an intimacy
of an enduring kind.

A Drop's Life

Just dropping now is a most difficult
Thing. To drop one time was an easy melt,
A frequent voyage, ice sears a hot shelf,
No bequest of pain, just another gulp.

But dropping now's so hard to recall
A trace of those shards of summer, a felt
Loss of civilization, infidel
With wrinkles clutched, a ship warped to coral.
Just getting out of bed, that sad affair,

Is too close to the wall, comes dropping low
In dawns when fog crowds the last night of earth

Fosters entry into another air
That old diaphragm of watery groans,
That dropping's complex through our time's own birth.

Rituals of Autumn

In pine needles there are psalms that haunt.

Small pine cones try on those details
Of sugars, assume a permanent pose.

In this light Quetzacoatl is more than legend.

Some leaves are spotted with rust color, their chemical bonds
In transition propositioned into homeless facts.
Through each rendition of "it's time to flow"
They translate themselves from protein.

They do not mime the season; they *are* the season.
Occasional breezes sway the maroon ones, those
Inclined to chanting "kyrie eleison"
Amid the chimes of clinging.

A brief relief in this climate of reality,
They too will blend in like footprints from the Eocene.

Silver Lake
(Kit Carson Lodge, California, summer 2004)

I've been here before. Years ago.
Peopled, camper-friendly,
angled spray-peels of jet and water skiers.

To the northwest, a mountain, volcanic,
massively gray-purpled
corners the horizon.

Firs reassert themselves
by growing from crevices of
mammoth slabs of granite.

Not even a whisper of a cloud,
only jet trails.
Dead pines bone-bleached gray
resemble fish skeletons
against lush enclaves of forest.

In the evening, after sundown,
"Your Cheatin' Heart" beats from a radio
as does "Party Doll" and "The Great Pretender."
It is Kit Carson Lodge, circa 1957,
all over again.

Red Leaves on a Gray Day

Outside leaves bend slightly, quaver in the breeze.
Green deepens, darkens into red, browns

With each movement.
The day grays, wet. Seasons murmur, pine limbs
Steady yet at the same time dance.

Peace grows cold as a child
Cries at clouding skies.
Green darkens, deepens the autumn hour.

Pines vibrate into undiscovered hues.
Red leaves on a gray day course through
Summits that resound within the sound
Of all returns, upraise the soul
Scale noted heights and unearth
Words divined closest to the breath.

Processional

Now the flux crashes,
clicking fires among the running blood.
These margins of seaside sky
celebrate summer:
whitecaps surge and scroll,
dorsal fins on a blue-green sea.
Spidery arms of kelp
shiver in emerald shadows.
Gulls play tag with fleeing shadows
dancing on wind-slicked grass.
Eucalyptus trees sway in every direction as if
to say it is holy just to be.
Harbor seals flipper their way
through a periodic surface.
Joy collects here in this summer of earth,
blazes hatched from wild innocence.

Hate Clubs

They
hate green,
They
hate bright,
They
hate dark,
They
hate light.

They
fear love,
They
urge hate,
They
die dead.
Clubbed
by hate.

Sunset, Russian River

In these yellow eyes the sun
        is dying
as over this fragmented world
        a hush
yawns amid the ceaseless falls
        of flow.

Into arcs of each daring
        cast
there shoot gray-glints of line
        for
fishermen are patient, their
        virtues

pensive, primeval,
        lie
deepest in the throat.
        They
will not catch the sun
        whose

reflections become dancing
        gods
rising slowly across the river
        into set.

Muir Beach

note the edge
where seawinds open into song and
still cows graze the greens
where breakers scarp profiles
their crags sprayed foam-snow;
a lone cormorant cruises

rolling shoulders, his eye
a razor for the lurk of wave;
out a sea a tanker lingers
and lingers
in the sunset setting
where cloud billows tint
eyelids of seem and
journeys west, the east to steep;

in a deep inlet a mallard
feeds, his head dips down
· below the edge
where song scatters waves
of curvaceous now

The Ends of Summer
(Del Rio Woods, Russian River)

The beach
has died, that annual sadness.
Only the breezes snake buoy by buoy.

Lifeguard
snoozes with one eye open. Green now
autumns through yellow bamboo.

Late suns
pass over new ends of the dock
among voices lulled and jaded loves.

Sunshades
peer so faded; our lifelines gray
in moving hands; tied canoes sway.

Hawks drift
aloft, awaiting the dead meat
of lovers in the yellowed oak.

Nothing
remains save memories that fly.

Sonoma Mountain

Lying on the couch barely
conscious, these memories
slip and keep slipping
back to the top of
Sonoma Mountain.

What innocence!
Like shooting metaphors.
Picking wildflowers
firm in their yellowy wisdoms.
Clutching them
with such runaway
tenderness
as though we could
undo dying and death.

And your hushed eyes
in their philosophic bones
kept asking, borne
with a kind of rage and
outstretched wonder,
how many springtimes
you had left.

Until we wound
back down the trail
and mingled with those
maybes once again,
no answer rose.

A ranger said we could
not take the flowers home.

So we tossed them like chips
high into the flames
and higher into the riddles
of this twilight.

Del Rio Woods

No clouds. Just blue.
And two solo pines.

Just then
with no one looking
the unconscious lifts
its ocean to the surface
and with its secret
sticky fingers
beckons past bikinis and bread
to a genesis. To the
inaudible mantric sound.

No blue. Just clouds.
And two solo pines.

Embracing Metaphors

Unclear jellyfish in the reeds I am,
That mighty zero, primal astronomy.
Your disappearing fact, an atlas in stages,
A phrase within a phase, my blue fountain:

This collection of cravings, one last kiss,
An extended family in ecstatic prayer.
I'm in transition, a ghost perky in levitation,
A melody within a malady.

Women at the Russian River

"Sorta cigar shaped," she urged.

"Go get the ball, Orbis," said another.

"A twelve year old kid, imagine that, he got religion
and melanoma."

The Irish Setter emerged with a green tennis ball
and shook his fur.

"Are the knower and the known one?" she asked,
directing her sunglasses into the shades.

Little Jonathan mopped his curls and asked
over and over "Are you happy, Mom?"

Joni adjusted her halter. A speck greened across
the sky; Orbis leaped the waves.

"You know she died for love, honey."
With her body still browning,
Joni continued to glean
from that novel yellowing
shapes of her sounding yen.

Shasta Reflections

Fishing Lake Siskiyou with its silent ripples,
A bald eagle soars outward in a circle,
Spies a fish near the lake's surface skin, and swoops with
Talons golden poised and lifts its catch up away
Into the summer dawn.

Deep shadows of forests indent the folds
Of hills that wake up reluctantly as the sun's light begins

162

To penetrate first by tree tops gradually illuminating
Lower branches until their entire length is bared.

A domination in purple, Mount Shasta looms
With remnants of winter's last snow, rivulets of
Volcanic accents now even in late summer.
From the quiet of this morning on the lake
Shasta's unveiled, unchiseled, scarped dominion
Turns my blood into an ecstasy for wilderness.

Homing Napa Valley

In my father's 1940 Ford, plodding north
Beneath skies of steel blue
I lounged on the front seat, listening
To the coos of a dozen pigeons twitching in the trunk.

Always this trip seemed the same:
It evoked atmospheres from a hymn:
"Abide with me, fast falls the eventide."
Only the times were different.

I cherished the pink-reds and reverend purples
On harvest vines as we passed oak-scattered hills
And imagined galloping horseback from groves to graves.
Passing wineries without hype and domains of tourists,
We discovered poetry ripened untouched
Until christened by the spoken word.

The trunk, tied with rope, contained a crate
With racing pigeons: Stassarts, Sions, and Bastins.
They were clocked in their homing flights, especially
The two named "Invincible" and "Pearl Harbor."

On a road in crisp October, we pulled over.
Off came the rope from around the crate

With its reddish, blue, and gray aces eager
To shatter records. My father opened a little door.

In his tanned hands, he held "Invincible," carefully
Peered into her tender eye, checked the silver
Band on her leg, and with an upward sweep
Tossed that pigeon toward the sun.

Wings flashing, she compassed for home,
In direction directed, climbing in circles as if waiting
For the next one to be cast like shadows across
My eyes. As if from a dream all found release.

Each spanned the firs and pines beneath cirrus skies.
Soon they resembled furrowed eyebrows, sequins
On a sulfur-orange horizon; they outwinged us.

They soared for home where eucalyptus trees swayed.
In the pigeon loft a timer recorded their times.
Lightning in flight, they became veterans in the ways of return
That cruised beyond even real numbers.

In Sacred Woods

Alone, near this clearing's light clearing,
there's a mind to explore these sleeping weeds,
ponder pensively and
note every cloud of waking love.

Given time, it is easy to understand this score
of sprinklings in the sun,
these incantations of solitude.

Here one may listen to the plum ripening,
current plays of wind and rain,
water running from nowhere,
and umber festivals of wood on wood.

Love

as it
recedes
along a

thinning line

the taste
of overripe

mirages

Summer Shorts

Windmills turn a
sparkling sun
leaves reaching out.

~

Fire trucks, gray goatees
freedom in cartwheels
milk drops, mustard dogs.

Clowning Janus

1.

Beneath plush palms
your soul waters

a heart of winter
when desires of snow

almost brave
tropical seas:

you flame north
and so engrave
a sonnet
to wintry truth.

2.

Winds of ice and
snowy mountains
make dyings
your restless search.

Even now
in biting cold
you flame summer

and lionize
in each miracle
the sun's storming blood.

For Robinson Jeffers

You there with your curmudgeonly axe
foaming at civilization's throat:
What can we say of your indifferent, cosmos-naked god,
your furies, our nemesis,

Circling, always circling hawk-eyed, like an electron
to peck out the eyes-heart of the human breed?
What? Have we breached the covenant
to hasten a craggy, rock-red oblivion?

You there with your freudian axe
gulp down your own fury's brimstone cup
you who prophesy out of the orchestra of greek tragedy
through a darwinized, seed-split calvinism.

Love Lost Tastes

like a postmortem sample
an autopsy performed
premature for want
of a widening vision
dreams
an ever afford
that even when floating
face down
through a thousand kitchens
of pain
there is still in those craving
lungs
snow-maned fury's air,
and in the sky's pink-orange-illumined face
horizons alive
that explode through
dead water

Stargazing

Fireworks pulsing. Between stars,
Fixed on nothing, the fire.
Inside black holes, with their hidden certainties.
The stars. On this hill this summer night
Orion mounts Pegasus, feeds the bear.
Izanagi tangos with Juno. Medea waltzes with Romeo.
Village greens thread through blue dwarfs and red
Giants from Clontarf to Shanghai to Tierra del Fuego.

On this night the heart contains
More than words. For one moment the butcherings
And injustice, the loveless in empty
Faces, the way winter courses through shivering blood—
These measures free fall, desire away.

We warm to this breeze, feel paradise and its unattainable
Shores, its rock-ribbed departed finally
Practicing aloneness
Through the whole point of their nativity.

The Native Returns

After so many winters, the summer's
Sun swims these worn hands and brightens the wine-
Shouldered hills. Coming home, no more going
Far, far away, I bring these memories
To a living end, one to remember.
A horseshoe tops the door of knotty pine,
Still exiles fortune's shade. Yet home's steep climb
From the past presents some memoried signs:
Eucalyptus odors, moss-ancient oak—

Once were these lost. Now nostalgia's sired
Eyes find poppies on a hill's leafy bed.

Such roots consume me, for they are love's yoke
Where all's remembered as strangeness desired.
After so many winters, winter's dead.

Amenities

Her needles move now by instinct.
Memory's threads over memoried tread.
A patchwork between what is
In the cards
And secondhand gossip
Like the olden days
She still beholds.
Yet whenever her needles pause
As though suspended
There's a curious lethean air.

She remembers how it was
Some years ago out watering
The easter lily and the ash
When she partly unraveled.
Her eyes they dimmed
Only to disclose
A face strangely
Gentled. She remains
In yesterday's mold.

Her children have dropped by since.
And both times, no
Just once, they fought
Over the price of selling her
True estate.

Still she holds to the golden days.

A kind of peace with bygone griefs.

Her fingers are now moved
Not by whether
It rains or clouds, but
By instinct and that alone
Along those threads that thin.

Cracking the Sun

A poem's roar opens a vortex,
yesterday's ink of tints
that makes perception
assume a future's helix
where music swells what
the unsaid tells
moving through moonstruck lines.

Devouring borders, poetry's craft
unconsciously comes into itself the way
a current yaws. Teasing mindscapes
with a ballade of reckoning, it grasps
the throat, spits flame into fire,
and goads forenoons into a gloveless shaking.
It burns to burst cloudbursts
and in a desert's arid moment cries:
"Bring on your thunder dreams,
string up that Dionysian lightning,
let's crack the sun in two!"

Having paid an exacting price—
a harrowing by fire and frost, that
bevy of questions in winter's light,
a bearing of flesh to retouch the unborn—
it earns insight with an unarmed genius.

A Colt Pauses at the Spring

In your slick brooding waters
Skies sail with a primordial silence.

The spotted colt begins to drink and pulls back,
Startled by your veteran loneliness.

Once again he drinks, then pauses,
His wondrous eyes opened wider.

He cannot fathom your unfathomed pools
Whether it be in the centuries of childhood

Or your naked remembering mind.
There you no longer embrace the illusion

That history's thirst only gathers with age
Or pants for a summer season of the imagination.

Hark

How you bled and I, your mother, wept
For the times they spat on you
And speared you and mocked your
Passion. Even the way they brought you
Down. Draped across my legs your body made me
Seem younger in Michelangelo's *Pietà*.

Since then have I heard them regard
Your appearances as occasioned magic, your bearing
· Royal among the poorest, your astral body
Projections seated cross-legged on the Ganges
Where some say you became a radical
With Hindu *darshan* who could still the waves of the eternal
Now. Another commoner with messianic pretensions
Who bestowed on existence the will to meaning.

Another state convulsing with a millenarian proclamation.
I, for one, with maternal instincts, knew just
Barely what you could do. At Cana.
With Lazarus. Stretched on the tree. Poet and
Sailor of despair, morningstar of our first awakening.

From such intimacy with God, deepening even reason's
Chatter and meditation's gaze, how could I in a million
Mother tongues ever doubt nearly unimaginable you?

Dreaming Airs

Overhead
Honking in formation
Fleet geese span.

While city-bound and job-tired
I gaze at what I shall someday
Free when wish invites deed.

Sammy

Littler than most of the litter,
smaller than most
of his tribe when fully grown,
and while my daughter and son still sleep,
with paws outstretched,
he crawls into the shifting shapes of slanted sun
that, faster than a snail's fate, quietly
move across the floor.

As each patch climbs the downside of innocent beams,
slants with fingers spread across the legs
of a living room chair,
he waits until the sun resumes
coverage of the floor's colder face.

He seems to sense, perhaps by the shortness of his
cross-bred memory,
perhaps by the resolution of his elysian fields
hunter instincts
just how brief summer is
even in the sun.

dogs scamper
as couples embrace
the beach wind shifts

Naked

That's how it feels
standing on
these emerald waters
surrounded by diamonds.
Touching my cut lips,
cut by saying your
sacred name, a medium

no one after all
is quite able
to fathom.

All I sense
is your unimaginable
high renaissance
pursuing these bones.

I dance and dance
and fall into your paradise.
And from such emptiness
I breathe the cool
moonlit silences, gaze
into a pool-blue of maybes,
and recall your delicious
awakening words:
have you forgotten
the unkillable love
that centers
the circumference?

Shooting Stars

Forty Mozart
lifetimes in a thimble—
no quicksilver copy
but real proof.

And there are long, yawning Methuselah lines often
distinguished
by being disinclined to count rhythm and turn off the sprinklers.

Three Epigrams

Might it be the black of your ivory hands
Is the ebony of your pearl's demands?

Is love a tomb with breath's unease
Which death may cure when time doth please?

Whoever you're screwing
Could be your undoing.

Sex and the Myths of Sex

Primal urges, innocents that careen into scarlet
consume our islands wild with desire,
undulating in their arousal
among sleepers shaken by shook flames.

On dark evenings as seawinds breathe
through these islands and clouds,
desire enflames the cunning blood.

It is not only fishers of predawn
who remind us of these telltale lures
that ignite desire into a brightening scarlet.

Myths shape as whole families
trees that real history decays.

Shelve the myths for now. Make your focus the real
for within the momentums of curved time,
finally enfleshed
we remain.

The Lessons of Music

Chords hammer into blues time
While a baby explores the living
Rings of auroras about her.
A victrola's brassy mouth sits atop the piano
As the teacher positions
The child's fingers lovingly on the keys.

Everyday flutes explore motifs in metronomes,
Soulwise truths between beats.
Lily leaves reach out and almost compose the stuffed
Rabbit whose ears pirouette past steady woodwinds.
A dated clarinet assumes melodies within the
Strings of sleep, of guitars that play unplayed.

Two Raggedy Ann dolls rest in flowered
Blouses against volumes of migrant histories,
Each a mistress of whole tones.
Next to a portrait of the Milvian bridge in ancient Rome,
The breath of Bach follows itself like a fugue
Into a polyphonic canyon.

Our Sixtieth Reunion

Ponder it. Not too many years away
How survivors will have shrunk
Or ballooned in the shrinking light.
Even now pockets of attrition
Worm their way through the graying heart.
How we help one another. Finally!
And how passage razes the bodies of experience.
Each year does not seem so tall after all.
Simply being here, in the wakes of so much
Absence, ignites the miraculous.

Gone the days when cliques glared.
Gone the noons when crows' feet first smiled.
What gratitude we cradle for small appearances.

Retiring strengthens our refusals to let late summers pass
Uncoils our decks across, freezes profiles (made up
As far as made up can take us)—these we
Now rarely discern
A processional, a tide agelessly
Born to bear us

Past rage, past our poorer powers,
Through another serpentine
Passage that relives the past
To relieve our presence
But briefly.

Tournament Cup
(Spring 2004)   *for Katie*

Our daughter smiles,
her braces glint in the sun.
Her team has not scored but now
she dribbles
the ball toward their goalie.
Armed with a sure-footedness,
and long legs, she weaves
around two opposing players,
aims, and shoots. As the ball zings
into the net, past their
fallen goalie, pride and high-fives erupt
from our side.
She smiles as we cheer for her.
Though her team scores again,
As far as I am concerned,
in my naiveté,
Hers is the team's only
goal that game.

Sacrament

All is alive, everything's holy
Keeps time though times perish, flames deeper things
When burning through "yours" and "mine" solely.
Everything's alive, all is holy
When God's enfleshed with love's breathing only
Where mind's reckoning becomes one with one's king.

All is alive, everything's holy
Keeps time though times perish, flames deeper things.

Through Aging Eyes

How light curves about
Her arms and dying suns
Thread her eyes in
Twilight to close a rose.
Through snowfalls and trees
Creaking heavy above
White-whiskered avenues
She awaits by the fire
Summer's calm to attract her light.

Her noons unfold and crease her chin.
She waters long roses swaying beneath
Graying squirrels
Playing elm to elm. Even westerns
On Saturdays at that lonely
Movie house where each feature
Starts to end
Before it means to begin,
Are prayer wheels held fiercest
To the breast.

Each stroke of her brush adds
Character to her eyes and
Amorous arms on windblown sheets
Each sun a yearning to rise. Her skin colors
A sonata tone, her miracle a
Finite noon,
Her beauty remains uncharted
In chiseled stone.

Again, Love

Green is alive in springtime
Resurrections burst in daffodils.

Yes, love comes again,
The truest fire in winter

With sonnets undreamed
In lilies of genesis

That dares a kind of joy
Both essential and luminous.

For Sidney Lanier

Out of those prison amenities,
Still you escaped with your rhythm's song,
From such lung-filled extremities
Came poems through raven days long.

Out of that coughing, composing gait
To protest smoky factories' hell,
Your longing flute's anapestic mate
Borne by confederate days that fell.

Out of the red clay of Georgia's soil
With God's greatness within each song
Your symphonic poem yet lived to tell
Of the Chattahoochee flowing along.

Through a Glass Lightly

Jesu, like some newer Adam...
dead in blind, found in see.

(No stained glass on your nose for me!)

Illumination's blood runs through you
a peace within the sea.

Last of the Final Farewells

Although I will not see you again,
thoughts of you
linger in my fingertips
as the wake of your boat entwines
skies of us in sea swells
brushed with blue.

I stand up in the stirrups
as you gray on a graying horizon.
things seem lost as
my horse rears up and neighs.

Yet we know it had to end.

The meaning of silence
opens us
away from the ruins of contagion's midnight,
beyond seasons of a stygian plague
and winking lusts of the closed mind
when desire finally sees through desire.

Instructions for a Poetry Contest

Poems may be single-spaced or married
But blossom best when left unharried.

Unripe Apple

Crickets, autumn's twilight:
from your bequest at last—
self-conquest.

The Sublime

The mind's stillness, once near unfading,
Where waters sky-blue ran smooth, caring.

Amid summer isles, the silence
Where daring drew the angelic, ennobled.

         *

Directionless now: terrorists, summits apart,
Aliases, sleaze, hammering venom into our rude
Flesh, pre-apes mushroomed, do we really hug oblivion?

After the Leaves

fall, you can pass away
from that subway station
and the living dead surpass.

Poolside Shorts

Hand-in-hand
waiting for bodies
pool still serene

       ~

Grandpa's posture
does not betray
concern for his grandchild

Slaver: Looking Back through the Middle Passage

...the air soon became unfit for respiration, from a
variety of loathsome smells, and brought on a sickness
among the slaves.   —Olaudah Equiano

A slave ship's hold stuffed with body after
Body held whimpering, bound to suffering,

Squeezed by barbarity as when the mind
Closes, brandishes chains, the shapes in which

A hand at one moment caresses, flogs at another,
Writes histories in continents of blood.

Cruelty's shape uglifies, assumes freedom
Lies, makes the enslaver's enslavement

Complete in his own profit. Such whips prelude
Uprisings and jumps out of vomit and disease

Overboard into friendlier deaths,
Leaving the hold of the vermin behind.

One Spoke on the Wheel

Your pencil rests on a test
That tests as far as
Memory can reach.

And you first thought
It might just be or
Be not...so important.

It is only one spoke
On the wheel: Mary Shelley,

Mozart, wildlife management,

Hafiz, diverse ecosystems, Chuang Tzu,
Sacagawea, Plotinus, Paul Célan,
and you thought it was,
even without Renoir, so important.

Predators

Hyenas and cunning jackals pick the flesh
Of a slumped wildebeest
as elephant hunters
lunge for ivory or everyday flesh for lampshades

*

Then there are those octogenarians waiting
for a hip to mend
while the peoples' ambulance chaser
card in dispenser
awaits to file your complaint with citations
to authorities
and reasoned unreasons for settlements
they too may profit by

*

Funeral parlor heads, along with platitudes,
and vestiges of something eternal
reduce your dust to a hillside
urn or between waves with flowers strewn
as your will, probated, and followed with family
contests despite your no-contest clause...

*

The Kalahari, 120 degrees during the day carrion
yet lures the carnivorous culture of vultures,

the putrefaction of goodbyes picked clean

as

    though
    life
    was
    nothing
    sacred

*

That genocidal, devouring cannibal
ready to eat and show nuclear disdain
for his fellow human beings and has the
ignorance to call it honor in wars that marry dust to dust

*

Is all that remains the pawing of jackals
and the insidious laughter hyenas
etched on a soundless sky?

Going Alone

Kisses once real fade.
Yet you live.

Your heart's scars scar no more.

Beyond heartbreak and breathless romance
You search through all of those faces
For the one face
That connects all of the generations
Through tequila nights and arms
unarmed for loving.

No relation, only hazes flushed purple.
No caring, only posturing
As rejection proof.
Going alone, even lonelier.

So many lies, impersonal eyes
Hollow, lifeless, without compass.

At least your heart's scars scar no more.

Seeing You Again

Beneath wakening blossoms
your smile rises
behind my eyes and down
where perches the twilight heart
that at your touch releases me.

Beside evening ponds
whose lids close the skin of night
your hand floats,
beckons these angels
swells their pulse's logic
and steps into beauty.

So many partings, dust-spumed
in white heat's midsummer
relights a drowsy recollection
of our starry beginning.

A Greener Hill

Each May I hiked up that green hill to pick
A bouquet of poppies for my mother.

She loved their bright orange firelit clusters
And stamens that surfaced as though sunlit.

They honored her for dancing in her prime
With a gathering to offer her praise

In spite of her fast-dimming dated Mays.
And now in her felt loss, how dashed her times

Seem. Yet orange colors a higher light
Through old memories and ways that disclose
Clean as sacred fire beyond flesh unfolds
Beauty in what breathes to perish from sight.
Each May she walks and waves for me to see
When those past springs release her back to me.

The Man Who Never Fit

Easy rounds and compulsive days
        Of soapboxes and TVs
        Were not he.

He tried, yes he tried, he did
        He tried winters there and roots then;
        But he did not fit.

And the fits the townsfolk
        Fitted him for: salesman and bulleye
        Were not he.

The shrink theorized
        And the doctors hypothesized
        But their pictures were not he.

Dying early enough in life
        To starve in profits
        Was not he.

Job on job he tried
        Perhaps a marriage or two would do;
        But it was not he.

A misfit was his theme
        He sang as though stars were poems;
        And no one understood except he.

He explored a kind of love:
         To fit him with none
         Was the way his fit was finally one.

Soundings in the Old Wilderness

To hope, love, hear, desire, and hate
Are lost somewhere, sometimes late
Before one's still life in memory
On the smoothing shores of euphony.

Crashing breakers against rocks do pound
While one can still hear the sounds
Of a channel buoy clanging as it tips
And seagulls following white-sailèd ships.

Death Laughs

When death laughs among blue vapors
and your aging voice
declines as sooner-than-not sleep
blots out
the world's bleating,
let not your tears
overdo compassion's ecstasy.

Instead firmly anchor memories
of this brief passing
that formed

threads of our last setting
when these hearts allowed beauty no waning
of the infinite
but left intertwined lines,
the skin of our union, in wrists of foam.

Through Valleys

This legacy, these tears
not yet attuned to the hibiscus,
a world that comes
to nothing
and vanishes in dust dreams
yet affirms and redirects.

Mastered by sorted passions,
the heart's glass music
pulls us onward
through a thousand valleys

and edgeless uncertainties
until there's a disclosure
divined by wisdom
that our lives are endless
wanderings on the waves of paradise.

Journey to the Abbey of Gethsemani
(Trappist, Kentucky)

Let us now put out those fires
and let the holy one begin
in bells, beauty, and song
prayers whose vigils in us
sacred breathe.

Here the word endears the silence.
Silence, the sweetness of being there

at one at last with the one.
Let the mystery of holy fire begin:
beauty out of fire makes bread
bred for flights
of the alone to the Alone

for the divine by silence releases
bone by captive bone.

Farm View, Late August

Clay cliffs distance eucalyptus
branches; cows gaze as a pink mist craters
into a dreaming mouth; day's
labor wearies; this summer's hills yellow to brown
as a.goose laments the loss
of her gander; Rome did not fall in a day;
phone lines lend a chilly silence in this last light

A Poem Found

We are not
meant
for empty plastic
in the dankest times
or ash-basted paste
but a genius
for ecstasy
through the subtlest vibration
where wilderness flows
and discloses nectar
for the journey of return

summer hills rise
a boat rolls —
tules sway

*

the sun hides in dunes
as waves prance
a fishing boat sways

four ducks ride the ripples
as the tide rises—
gulls glide by

*

barefooted kids
watch gulls eat chips and grapes—
puppies barking

The Drive to Chaos

That vase by your window is
the rain. When thunder pounds

and rattles the pane, the vase leans over,
as if drawn to the windblown sheets of rain.

It crashes on the floor and shatters,
obeys the laws of physics and karma.

Inside, in the mind's rainblown trees
chance plays with limbs that bend and snap.

As you sprawl by the window, you realize how
landscape *is* mindscape, how mindscape *is* landscape
landscape and mindscape are one are one are one.

slow setting sun
pigeons cooing—
pages turn in the breeze

The Magic Globe

The blackness of the ink
purported to show every content:
from the cattail's rustle to the salmon's leap
to the emperor's masterful blade.

You asked:
If the butterfly flits across the ocean,
will the emperor still sleep well?

And then:
If geese in flight inspire, will dragons survive?

I smiled as the answers rose to the surface:
The emperor sleeps well; his mind yet
resonates with imperial dreams.

Such words, descendants of the stones we sat on,
made us laugh; they formed our friendship.

Overhead, geese in V-formation spliced
the afternoon sky while on a leaf
a tiger swallowtail lingered.

The dragons survive though the geese
cast shadows on the hills.

Even as we played, poised by each stretch
of truth, we knew those words
concealed answers whose futures knew no end.

Graves

Old photos of you, of us,
happier days, not yet divorced
beyond recognition,

empowering complexion,
mirrors remembered.
I carried them to the garbage, sat back
and mused how lies informed your
truth that once formed
your words.
Trust's beauty died
flew with the flow
so long ago.

Requiem

Unlike gray dawns, this one emerged
black-throated in unforgiving blue.

White lips of earth
formed a band of vinegar.
addiction to visionless avenues,
storming fists.

Like membranes
this one opened sheer in the searing heat.
It revealed nothing except
nothing hallowed when you
tried to exile the divine
in you.

At Least

Europe lets her churches fade scenically
and does not rob them
of their robed beauty.
Antique chants, hymns of grandeur's God.
sprung rhythms of ancient memories
of the race overgrown
with vines &
a solitary sunflower

echo somewhere beneath
the songs of hurry, hustle, and haste.

Yet the sun warming,
the longing of birds
also rises in winter,
ministers to something beyond appetites,
and bearing questions that matter
beneath skewed spines of the age,
forms again
despite the deserts of a
seemingly inescapable setting.

Sick Puppy
(to a fellow poet obsessed with suicide)

Stop whining
About your august love
Death with a capital D.

Must you glamorize suicide to rationalize your death wish?
Your fear of aging looks
And broken relationships?

Dorothy Parker survived several attempts:
Read her poem called "Resumé" for her qualifications.

Is life more "authentic" because you slash your wrists or overdose
On your friends? My friend, quit whining:
It only disturbs my dog who has her paws over her ears.

We all die in due course.
Just don't gussy it up with metaphoric sentiment and clinical crutches.
You have your own self-indulgent ennui to attend to.
Those martyrdoms of depression are not courageous:
Are they not the luxury of sedentary self-sorrow?
My dog is tired; she wants to bring her paws down.

The Magnetism of Water
(musings of a mere lad)

In their efforts to impress
local high school girls
get nose jobs,
take injections for thicker lips
pouting with pouts
to feint a sultrier hit
magnetically drawn to water burning,
even their pink and purple hair,
nothing rare, is fake.

Their grunts often mask but rude wants.

Yet the lifeguard has to watch them too
down past the erotic lines where
they are drawn and redrawn
to savor the saccharine with her eyes.

Saturday Dawn

Sadness. Morning's child.
Laundry in.
Day blinds, cocky sun.
Love, an elder theme,
Metronome that waves in rain and cheekbones.
Soap. The regular motions.
Even lunch casts into fantasies.
The center implodes—all our networks—into broken.
Yet there in the mind a dusky avatar:
Touch and live. Your music rings it back.
Chords that retrieve.

Traces

Your voice soothes,
founds a heart
your grace elliptical,
a prophetic sadness—
streets left blue
with sinking loves.
Do we weave
only memories out of all
we say and do?

Desert Storm

a hawk's wing flapping blackness
ignites the silence
into quiet storm

Home of the Unexpected

Elysian fields and sweeter dreams. Then
reality throws the moon in a marsh.
And this despite your creative best.

There are realities in the sun
you did not consider:
ancestral lines of convex hands,
clocks melted into dazzled fish,
horses rubbed with love,
incandescent flood plains,
ages dripping with honeycombs,
making rhythms into thickets of riddles.

Such realities, adjusted for uncertainty,
may be wired, may be almost unexpectedly
cornucopias where the brain
has a mind of its own.

To My Father
(after the night of turning cold)

A final meeting. Mom returned from
Tennessee to learn of the pain
You would not reveal, only complain of.
Thirty-eight years of marriage
About to snap. She expected you
To be around; she lived
For your presence, even a ghostly one.

She rose
From her own heart's failure
Just to be with you.

And now you slowly lowered
us all into stone.

Chaos stirred the air.
The scent of death waxed stronger, cancerous
Visits came like labor pains in the night
Until blood filled your lungs
And you were gone.

She too was gone, a romantic
Nursed on old memories that refused to burst.

Months later, she too cast off
Out of longing for you,
For the ghostly romance of you,
Beneath the still ground of you.

Sunyata

These poems dilate empty
breath.

Into heaven I reach
by loving
in this flowering
emptiness.

Changing Diapers

Appearances never ending.
Signatured as the seasons.
Lived cries, kicking feet
Perceive more than oiled hours.

How subtle light mortalizes our looks,
Gestures of the busy hands,
Expectant intrusions
Gifted new life,
The true ones, forever born.
Dryness or wetness chanced by change
Regular as untocked hours.

The Message of Massage

These muscles taut
along the spine
fingers curve into dunes of flesh:
they could pull a trigger
in a crowd or
host a communion exploding up limb and lips.

The heel of hands circle bone on bone.
You groan over arcs of stress and elbow turns:
there's a moan rising

like a lover's eyes
beneath ribs
concentrated as the only steel
you have
against this marauding press.

Raise the heel: your geography
stretched into biographies of bone,
memoried muscle, a tear in the island finitude.

Everything depends on loosening,
this finger urging
along triceps, anatomies of the closest message.

Awakening

When you needed me most,
I was sleeping.
The fish had already fed.

To hear talk about love
As though it is sugar-lined.
It is always listening, waiting,
An angling so silent it surprises
By how fast it can go.

Storms

The Russian River a green calm this a.m.
Umbrella stands poised in its yogic wisdom.
A red canoe tied still to last summer.

One boy cannot stand the calm.
He thinks nothing is happening in his season's unwinding.
Rock after rock he throws but does not see
Past the duration of splashes.

I am trying to decide whether to dive in.
The river greets all green and calm, easy on the flesh.
Its coldness invites, its vision hollows out drums
Of sky. I relearn as I enter
A music of solitude, storms of position and process.

On Seeing Our Daughter

for Katie

in the womb at twenty weeks
Your screen debut pauses me:
there's wonder at our frailty,
your instinct for this forming bone.

We find you as you, us:
eyes, mouth, limbs, and all:
gathering thrums of storied beat:
measures all type cast, typical—
yet ours.
With technology to make us wonder,
you expand our world:
we gasp at the intricacy of yours.

Your lenses illumine the clarity of water.
We see you dressed in lanugo,
your miraculous body kneeling
into the visible.

You turn in your turn
your undressed rehearsal
for these alien winds
your smile riddles,
gazing dark-eyed
into this peopled air.

We await your heart dancing
in colors of this earth.
We wait to celebrate you
with gratitude.

Some Friends

there are cannot help
but disappoint. Even beneath
summits undefiled by cravings.
They just can't help themselves.

Maybe because of misremembering
your sympathetic eyes
on some lonely boulevard
when their loneliness peaked in
an isolated dark.
Maybe because not understanding
you mean what you say
thinking you only say
what you won't mean

as if deep down you half
expected them to be someone
else who would assume the courage
to stand with you when you stand alone.
Not someone prone to lying
who shifts a stance like a split second weathercock.

Nor a Dr. Jekyll half-life, haunch of
aped desire, who expects with
accustomed smirk to upstage the final
wrinkle in another's life or sparring
with delusion's throatiness to take
the next bus to isles of the blest.

Deliverance

The mothered truth in your coming:
Delivered in the wait of anxiety, our expected wish.
Through the birth canal a socratic midwife
Divines parabolas of soul.

Through dimming acquaintance
With the rich particulars of paradise
You can scarcely recollect
How parabolas almost touch the infinite.

It is not easy to remember the infinite line.

There is mortared truth in your coming:
Again you begin to babble in a universal tongue,
Veins that connect us
As though all you had ever lived for
Returned us to the splendor of the simple.

Sneaking Chocolates

It starts with brushing my teeth or
Washing dishes. These cravings:
I have to guard against them.
They can overtake me.

That's when I have to get within myself,
Allow a cadence to flow,
To forget me down to the last
Line, a syllable pronounceable
At last.

Running on Empty

Engine hums and hums
cuts blades path over path
into convergent lines.

Vibrations
sensitize my hands,
become beatitudes at every turn.

My breath deepens
sacred shadows beneath branches
over tall grass along the walk.

Soon I'll be running
on emptiness where the hum is refined
but not by intention.

Hunger

Hunger gnaws at your name, sex, your health
Not to mention the amber haze of experience.
Here at the dump there *are* biased texts.
Authors and their art evaporate
While relatives are bounced out of breadlines.
Harassed by rats, worms eat the eye.
Accusation reigns.
Maggots devour purpose
As grief is punctured by shootings
And art of the state repression lines.
Thought does not escape the morgue.
Confusion ends in the mad house
Where privacy vanishes
As claws work to rip the last rinds of human dignity.
Ribs cracked here and there deny the truth
While sanity affirms the relativity of wards.

Blessed
for Marge Foley

while others feverishly chase rabbits
and rock their bloodied boats with every lie

you translate goodness into deeds
and spread your karmic blanket across the sky

and find easter in each blade of grass

poetry in the hummingbird
haiku in the poppy's eye
and engaging wisdom
in listening to mountains grow

Incomplete Stages

We are many though one and in between
Curtains reveal our directions on stage.
From ballad to acts, finales to comedy,
We ad lib shape, break a thumb
For fictive enchantments
Of the player's sun.

We come on with shadow scenes,
Clown and king recalls, tragicomedies backstage,
Directions nearly unspoken.

Your makeup is not
A variation of mine; you craft your exits too.
We might get together
At one stage, you a butterfly, I superman,
In a climate of love, a campaign of close shots,
Fiestas of engagement, straw hats, tragic rubbings.

Or not at all.

Our loves cast their own hues
For here and there are dreams curtains rise upon.

Some Say Poetry is Not

Heaven-sent
That nothing divine animates
Interstices of the brain.

What, pray tell me,
Do these prophetless, visionless, passionless
Procurers of austere pseudoscientific propositions
Know save the arrogance of their
Reductive theses and state-formulated pieces?

Wedding Poem

Graced with fire and passionate resolve
to live heart by heart
may your wedding joy be a part
in the reckonings of all your days.

For you, neighbors and friends, are wed
every day as a flame
that does not die in wind or rain
but enamors with the
flow of your changing faces.

Graced with fire and passionate resolve
in all your days you can discover
understanding and this uncover:
together you can allow
each to be
and with that allowing
love one another more
as a fire rises
in understanding hearts.

For married minds, truly married,
are by freedom unbound
through that divine ground
composed heart by heart.

Murder Death?

How shall we murder death
In the forenoons of lakeside solitude
And explore the unfathomed earth,
This honeycomb of recollected dreams,
While we are here
And not just die from there being no exit at all?

In the reenactments of dying
Carry nothing for the journey:
Not even the voices of wild ducks,
Pocketfuls of postmodern eyes,
Or conversations with a bluff's new moon
For there are those who have faith in death.

One might say only vision that risks can free us,
Furnish us apocalyptic lines with

Impulses of a higher self
Who passionately envisions a divine present
Without any limits
And refuses to remain pregnant with false dawns.

No Circular Craving

We have moved
From life seen as not merely
Circular craving
But bliss engaged.
We find suffering
At any place on the wheel.
Let your tears voice those griefs.

Yet interwoven at our backs,
Joy frees from its very tethering:
Out of joy in being, just being here now.

Your Eyes

for Rita

Your eyes, flashes of hazel,
a tilt and dazzle of hair
and neck, a smile
as wind curved
lifts into light
among the trees and awakens in me
your touch.

Your fingers long and longer
beneath my hair, your lips
beckoning my strength
meeting yours, a phoenix vision
arising together
out of
silence.

Erosion Snows, Late Afternoon

Draw your expectations
   in the eddies,
thread them through
   flowered mistrals
with your name cascading over them;
   try this truffle:
every shooting star needs dust.

Set your standards high but not
   so rigid they become faults
living on a diet of bluffs
   or overcast moraines;
striving is worth the vying
   until it becomes
a kind of dying
   amid unresolved mizzles of fog.

Playmates

You there, with eyes shaped like grieving triangles
with stages of the city in them, I am with you.

Let your tears mingle
With seas of the misunderstood.

Your sobs, let them blend in one roar.
This sadness can and may deepen.

You have but sampled the samurai appetizers,
Compassed bloody at points

Urged on by natural love.
I will be there as well, my rose of Jericho,

When you have taken in, and not only charmed,
More than any errant heart can stand.

New Directions

In a moment
there is a moment's bearing
that can still
the whitewaters of fortune.

The way peopled currents meet
with unseen reaches
beneath a passionate hub of stars.
The waterline too

hints at an unforeseen channel,
its aim settling on drift.
Lines of absence
appear sometimes to connect
the all in all

in luminous flesh.
Take you and I:
late summer, meeting you.
I expected nothing,
least of all this communion
bordering on lyrical bronze.

It is then I feel
in this body's curved time
magic of the providential,
a miracle in the revival of reversal.

One day we shall cease

explaining away
and begin to hear
what the silence has to say.

Sounds of Summer

Sounds of summer swimmers:
memories thread
such brevities—
characters formed
stroke by stroke,
all in breezes
that underwater hum.

Through the Kitchen Window

Tacos slow bubbling in oil, bowls
of chopped green onions,
lettuce tossed with sliced cheese,
sauce red in the pan,
the Buena Vista of time after turmoil.

Outside a gull stalks the morning-clipped lawn
   and finds what she has been looking for.
No longer does she peck
   an empty bag of chips.
She too persists in the way preparation prepares.
   Soon, in the dark circulation of an eye, she glides
off, targets this time a rainier horizon.

Evangelists of Greed

Never mind what Jesus said.

Gold-plated toilet seats
bring on the rapture.

Limousines chauffeured:
plots to assassinate,
fleecing lambs,
a business weaving
samsaric wool...

Money changers changing
hands
                  And more...

Never mind what the Buddha meant.

You See My Arms Open

I say this before all that is your world:
a fortress-fiefdom in Sweden,
blue bull tracks threading autumn,

one who needs proofs to love,
the puppet plays of Chikamatsu,
stone breakers in weatherproof boots.

You see, I become nothing but
a gravitational collapse
in time's cracked rigging-shells,
an ice crystal sleeping with uncertainty
a kitchen god nestling in the void,
or a river flowing into a nethermost wind
until I am with you.

So, you eater of ashes, fling those proofs aside
and open your mind too long asleep with death;
learn to breathe the way love sets free
in undying light
and needs no proof
in a country of spectator snow.

The First

for Claire Mirabile
my second grade teacher

Madonna. That's what I felt
at seven. You taught me
arithmetic, language, art and
more: me about me and how
beauty assumed human form.
To you, I was a boyish smile.
To me, the sight of you slowed
with supernatural light.

Your raven hair, tan suede
coat, playground whistle I
came to adore. I'd lean my
head on your shoulder during
reading and smell that powder
forever on your hands. You
were so proper: you always
smiled when you blushed.

The gold necklace you wore,
strung with dignity, enchanted.

I had never cared much for school
until I met you. I usually
preferred to swing high or play
hide and seek. Even reading
became surprising joy.

You were the first I gave my heart to,
only I didn't tell you then. And yet
it must have shown in every touch.
My heart felt as though a thousand
butterflies were fluttering at once.
Such effect you had on me.

Madonna. That's what I thought.

Later, when I read of Dante's adoration
of Beatrice and Petrarch's love of Laura,
I understood.

You were my moonlight Madonna arising
from mists of little boy dreams.

A crush? For sure. Infatuation? Naturally.
Yet when you kissed me on the last day
of school, I did not wash that cheek
for an entire week.
Even now, you are more
than a fondest memory
and so remain.

In the Steady Hum

In the steady hum of windshield wipers
The weather roots its mission:
To uncover love's grounding
That does not lose itself in fields of love-lies-bleeding,
Does not exile moods of signs,
And does not forge pearls of smoke.

It embraces trails of the divine,
Opens textures of rebirth,
And happens in the syntax of color.

The weather rearranges auroras,
Reads riddles first and finally overtakes
Elevations of bluebells, the soft rock of euphony.

Across the Canvas

Time's thumb rolls
oozing daubs of green haze,
rustic blues, reddish anger until
they discolor the sheep and the jet.
At its most alive, it whittles
a melee of village lives,
hands that shape white mountains,
sun slants from plucked stars,
pangs of unseen heralds,
art that invents persimmon silences.

Detour and Frolic

Frolic amid flowers grown high to the waist,
Wine still desired wet on your lips
This mustache seduced by the sun remains
Flecked with raspberry juice
This loving remembered behind the clouds.

Daisies smile when death cannot touch
Springs that release in us April's eyes
Even from love's parted lips
As sunflowers observe us
With stains of love in a sweet grassy patch.

kite floating over the beach
people disappear
in yellow fog

Two Monks

One monk says to another:
"Is time's transparence as joyous
as the look in that solitary heron?"

The second replies:
"Yes, as joyous as that shadow-dawn
I live as borrowed rain."

At that moment they also noticed
a bird-of-paradise and just knew
without saying a word.

Lake Tahoe Moves
(Summer 2004)   *for Ricky*

Our son is playing chess
against himself
on both sides of the board.
Already he
has beaten me
twice. (Not bad for a ten
year old!)
Maybe he will
outplay his opponent.
Someone has to win.

That is how most games
are set up.
It might even be his best side.
I smile,
continue to write this poem
as deliberately
as chess moves
with the endgame
in sight.

Moonflower on the Verge

There is, in this narrowing plot,
Much that lives never to bloom.
Or fits of kin, offshoots near to you
Who spread their glories on almost any morning.
Instead, you, white and glowing
In the purpose of moonlight,
Surrounded by sleeves of seeds,
Live to bloom but once.

In such an intimate exposure
What opportunity you have
At whatever prime point on the vine—
Whether a trumpet-shaped flower,
Heart-shaped sightings through weeds,
Or a profile in transience—
You can dare
And with a perfumed flourish,
Bloom to be adored
Even by the air.

Death in the Afterthought

To earth this afternoon
Crashes these already fragile assumptions:
Death is the end of the dream;
Parrots are either blue or green;
You always lose the way;
Hawks are more daring than blue jays;
Losers remain losers;
Guilt is worse than enlarged livers;
You must live in order to die;
Hades always defeats Poseidon;
Jack-in-the-pulpits outshine Queen Anne's lace;
There is nothing beyond the beyond;
Ancestors seed kin and kith tête-à-tête;
Cruelty and inhumanity have limits;
And canebrakes grow only in the paths of flower girls.

The mind, becoming free, turns over assumptions
As galaxies devour them.

Hawaiian Punch

Resting on this lanai, I drink in paradise:
Petroglyphs more sacred than graffiti rubbings,
Mango orange leis of aloha,
Grazing quail, curious sea turtles,

Churches with calvinist closets, missionary arms.
Inclined fires of luaus,
Lush raindrops that hula into lariats of cowboys,

Towering King Kamehameha,
Mandarin stages that discover more moons around Jupiter,
Plots fought over shells of beaches and orchid lava,

Ukeleles imitating windward waterfalls,
The steady roar of ancient Hawaiian temples
Pele's volcanic scorching to melt Mauna Kea's snow,
Cardinals red beneath tangerine butterflies,
Buddhas festooned with black sands,
Mauna Loa and sugar cane unveiled

Papayas that can afford whalers off Lahaina,
The misty eyes of Queen Liliuokalani,
Outriggers that warm the waters of Oceania.

Bali, Alyssa, and Winda

Wind rustled the topmost pine tree branches
In the lazy haze of a sultry summer.
Bali, Alyssa, and Winda watched
As seven swimmers crawl stroked their way
Toward that bliss of the other shore.
They wondered why it was so important
For them to swim all that way.

Some collective memory may have lured them.
Or maybe a rebel voice now unheard.
Maybe some selfsame storm-flame of flesh
Exposed them to cadenzas of philosophy.
What is curious is that before they dove in
Their usual silence turned to talk of love.

Bali was not the first to appear dazzled.

Nothing More in Wonder

Than this day dawns, that
muscles move,
as a gift, a breath, however heady.

The sun brightens petals of poppies
and mountains in the woods
among hosts of wildflowers.

These are open secrets
unless there is no
discernment of the play in a leaf,
searing in the pine needle's roar,
the living altar of a droplet of water.

These are open secrets
unless one is dead
to the feel of wet grass, remains
unaware that sands silently flow, or
regrets days gone by without self-illumination.

this warm rock—
the sun
fades through the trees

Blue Dragons, White Tigers

I hold a cup of tea,
Sip a poem.

Mimicking sound,
Blue dragons begin to roar
As white tigers wrestle
With spaces between the rhythms.

In the breezes bamboo still bends.

Sweating Beads

Sweating fidgety beads,
You swear you are telling the truth.
Running with the speed of wind,

You swear you are going nowhere.
Maybe you should not swear so much
Lest you make of truth red wires dipped in green.

Why Moonlight is not for Sale

The moon fills the windows and nearly blinds me.
Slowly the hills lay themselves open in a cream-yellow hue.

A mellow sky overtakes this choir of crickets and
Curves of the evening breeze.

This is when poetry may return to the tongue,
Tribal chants and drums recalled as a subliminal clearing of the
mind.

Resolution
(upon hearing certain women in India
decide to abort *because* their babies are girls
and after reading between the sonogram lines)

Today I have resolved
to have our little girl,
another mouth to feed, yes,
to ruffle the cuffs of care.

Not because of what dowry
she might require,
or, more cosmically, how much
she might be worth
compared to little boys
on the market.

No, I am resolved
to have our little girl
and see myself
as blessed

by her intrinsic worth.
You might say I have acquired
a divine right by choice
beyond the common cast of mind.

Back to the Basics

Opening like a tulip,
The day's swells rise and fall, rise and fall.
Fresh sea breezes brush across me.

Though weighed down by scars, and knowing
The despair and misfortune of fortune's past,
A joy, however dimly felt, dwells in the fact
There are sea breezes at all.

Towards Greater Definition

Along the river and its silence
snow-gloved mountains dotted
with spruce and birch trees
watch as papers, photos, mindscapes
all try to define and redefine you.

But you outswim each root, each
bent knee, to catch a current wider
than your personal tragedy, the high
comedy of your spicy poses as
sunlight is sometimes caught
in scoops of willing darkness.

A Shift in Momentum

In the excess of private light
not willing to flash between branches of the evergreen
has driven me close to maddening desire.
Only now can the private harvest
the gold of going public.

Only now can the wind be felt
among the poplar leaves dancing new life
into ancient lore and unearthed devotions.

No longer lifeless as though stunned
into a seemingly deep sleep
the molecular brilliance
of the latest universe
gushes with intergalactic promise
confirming the wisest words
that can arise from a mind
deeper than sleep.

Smoke in the Wind
campfire smolders—
the stars overhead

~

sunlight
on the rock—
the stars overhead.

~

pigeons circle
a steaming roof
the tall cactus

What We Know

What we know of anger is
How it gnaws inside the way hate does
And how far we must go before we reach
The fathomless hellhound pool of its ignorance.

We are clenched in a web,
Skulls of our own weaving,
     And find how closely shadowed
We are by hell's ancient barks and blood bullets.

     Be angry, you urge,
Be angry at the earth and timepieces-covered-with-ashes,
     You who love to make music make
War against music's complacency.

     And you are right, your memory's
Obsession flags you. No one could say
     You are indifferent or bottled up
To the fact of your suffering.

     Nevertheless, we are collared
In nocturnes of anger and their allies
     Thanks to our own making,
Blasted this way, ripped that way.

     Anger urges angles that dishearten,
Remains smoldering and seething,
     Avoids compassion and realized wisdom
As its gnawing harries us round after round.

Today's tomorrow's past

     A wet chick leaves the shell—
True presents forgets.

               *

     cars moving
     in front of the mountains
     a player kicks the goal

               *

"Who is it?" "Who is It?"
Your divinity ripens
Springs with silence,
Seasons all.

*

Death and noise
A flower shot—
The no-mind's a resurrection.

Late Summer Lament

There you go, faster than those summers past.
Look, this turn too is your difficult path:
Spring leaves, green with spring, already thrown by
Unconscious passages, now hint of autumn
Reds and old undulating magnetisms
Of purples and yellows. You have breezed like
Those swift Basuto ponies in mid-flight.
Your woodlands and swimming hole eddies know
Galloping moons, late suns that rise aglow
With spells of summer runs, bluish rhythms
That explore God as beauty, and believe
Beside pools and these soon-to-be dead leaves.
Your waters cloud with gray bubbles of smoke,
Yet begin their returns through wintry floes.

Back Home

Back home, I miss the firs, birches and ponderosa pines.
Closing my eyes, I see the snow-topped mountain,
Hear the chatter of hungry jays.
From a long descent, we finally dwell in the city.
So many channels I want to sleep.
There is something sublime in wilderness

That clears away the underbrush, shaves
Adjectives close, prunes deadwood,
Makes the subtle more subtle in making plain.
Mythical as pomegranates.
Lemons dancing yellow, butterflies zigging
As meadows that zag.
Back home, with my inward eye, I recall
My natural home with birches, firs and ponderosa pines,
Snow-sloped mountains and lakes astir
With ducks and geese.

From the Train

The fields breathe one pink blossom,
wintry days seem past.
It is a time of presence
but only a glimpse of the real presence.

Note the daffodils swaying appassionato,
the violins' melodic wine, the magnolias in tune.
This is the easy time, a glance of presence,
but not the real presence.

Lakes consumed with time,
forests burnt down to ancient limbs,
ravines curve with arteries of vines,
complexions rush mile after mile.

The presence is real in any season,
this shooting star, any cactus, that jack-in-the-pulpit,
not just a reverence since no memory,
now or once and future, may contain it.

All at once the fool's paradise falls:
behold the real presence in the faces that you meet.

House on a Hill

There is a house on a hill where dreams may come true:
Where plum mysteries duplicate largely thin,
Where stone idols melt into cosmic relief;
Where idylls of sunsets caress the flesh and
Epic roots burst through sand.

There is a dream housed on a hill where all comes true:
Where desire breeds fire and a contrapuntal ear,
Where scores of wisdom leave burning psalms;
Where beauty's reeds make lamas of love and
Ribs that ache marry the land.

There is a hill in a house where dreams come true:
Where breathing in unison unfreezes still life,
Where mandalas of tears match centuries with troops;
Where family histories confess seascapes of sky and
Horizons plumb pastels in our span.

Native Spirit
(after Lakota, Navajo and Paiute singers)

The singing men beat the drum.
They are praying to the creator.

All four winds descend and the trout dance.

The singing women chant a dream song.
Their voices ascend like eagles.

Both the raven and the bear greet the boom in thunder.

The children hum a dream song.
To the creator, they are praying.

Birds of fire shake the lizard-blue mountains.

The singing men pound the drum.
Their voices ride upon a whirlwind.

On the Beach in Healdsburg

A lone crow flaps by the two-lane bridge,
a white truck reappears behind the trees.

Here there is no thick perfume of star jasmine
but of the spectacle of dancing poplars trees
along this turn in the Russian River
as it quietly flows to the sea.

Steady flows sound the overcast air,
smoothing knuckles
of what is otherwise a jagged summer.

Sages of the Mountains

Sages of the mountains
are married
completely to the mountains
in spite of
earthly desires
remaining with them,
the adorations of wildflowers
that follow winter's snow
and the distractions
of others on a path to discover.

Their eyes resonate
a kind of holiness
and a clarity
resembling an empty fist,
a grounding quality
within layers of deep meaning
that can open doors

with spinning syllables
tuned in beyond
these times
to unmake
time.

Sages of the Sea

Sages of the sea
adore every moon,
draw and redraw currents.
Their insight also attracts those elements
in the sun that lead to a clearing of the mind
where being takes on its own
breath instilled illumination.
Such clearing of memory's cage,
which teaches the ways of the sea
and how we can live on the land,
yields soundings of a deep forgetting
that gathers in a shoreline of clouds
and renders possible
resurrections through epitaphs.

Sages of the Sky

Sages of the sky
ascend with ambrosia
toward recollections
beyond where an albatross can fly
where you may behold
the infinite whole
where pie slices and fractions become illusions
(as though the infinite can be made up with bit parts),
that conjure up the nectar of truth
disclosed at leavening angles or
the way herringbone patterns are stitched jagged
and, along with appassionato incantations

that bring together east and west,
to affirm as also necessary
cravings in the dark.
Then can we watch all our setting suns
reborn with a floodtide of dawns.

Epiphanies

Sometimes, what appears is
a gusting wind's will
willowing through the grass.

The wind plays variations,
uplifts a magpie
flushed with black and white moods.

In the same wind in the same time
appear lovers who pause to listen
three trees down from a startled faun.

Postcards
for Rita

α.

Dearest, the night blooms radiant
in this room where stars
outline constellations
where blessings
flutter everywhere. And this a crossing over
from one side of this sphere, brain,
this furniture, to another where we feast
yes feast on the miracle of just glazed sunlight,
dragons smoking through our time blip by feverish lip.

β.

Dear, the incessant whir of the fan reminds me of a steady wind
in the pines. It has a sweep that bends to unending. How

strange to still be alive and in motion and in motion the way
currents shift their force and in a quiet thunder lead us into a
wider frame of deference. Already we can discern sunlit bays,
islands to be spotted, seasoning of the seasons, where a universe
of kindness may be tried everywhere.

γ.

Dearest, never mind why
spring perfumes the cherry trees, squirrels leaping
limb up to limb, gold outdoing golden, or
memory deepening night.
One thing touches
the fingered instant: voices above water,
my life here with you, yes
a hunger when the lover blossoms in the lover.

What May Become of Us

At the Prado Museum, onlookers ponder the eyes
of Saturn devouring his children.
Eyes of horror, a nuclear family's fear,
as each one is gobbled up.
Goya underscored the paradox of cruelty,
how it undercuts the veneer of gloss,
the monster in each of us, trying to escape
unknown terrain only to be swallowed,
by the terror of the mountain,
sometimes whole,
for the time being who we are:
the contours of mindscape where thoughts
marry each of the ground zero passions.

Open Season

the saddest lines
are hunting
joy in every island

Double Gift

God acts. The Godhead does not.
*

Where the creature ends, there God
begins to be. —Meister Eckhart

This summer dawn
dawns sky blue.
I drink from this empty cup,
watch a jogger huff by as
squirrels skirr over and around the pines.
On the still life mountain
there is
still life
wrinkled with rivulets of snow.

*

Sensing a persistent absence,
my mind drifts
toward Eckhart's wilderness,
the wilderness
of Godhead,
the source of God,
that recurs not as cerulean blue
but oneness,
a nothing without a name,
a desert
watered with bliss.

*

228

Purple lupines hold
their own
across that august meadow.
Coyotes no longer howl
in the distance as they did last night.
A hiker emerges
from the woods, another lover
of solitude.
A squirrel sits up and listens.

*

Eckhart's Godhead,
beckons in this
silence of solitude,
the solitude before sound where God lies
hidden to realize
the source.

*

The multifarious shapes of day take hold—
sunrise cross-stitches
the field
with its shades of wild grasses,
spider webs sway
in the sun's incantations,
a woodpecker
hammers staccato in the lemon solitude.

*

Being here now
may be
entertaining a double gift,

broadening vision,

realizing the eternal
now
finding more than a particle in each wave,
the dark night
beholding the unseen
which cannot be exhausted by words.

Wintry Winds in Summer

Things shattered in the shapes of sin
and majesty's reflections
are sometimes lost in the dead of midnight.

Yet we live through all this:
identities forged,
wars over thumbnails of land,
preventable sufferings,
frozen plains hardening our better halves,
the loss of friends
and slithering impulses,
not to mention the latest epoch of terror
imposed by those
who appeal to the worst
in being human
as though they could
never master their fears of insignificance.
A wintry wind in summer,
they spread their fingers across
human fate and kill in the name of this or that,
clouds emptied or rainbows hidden-away.

Lakeside at Nightfall

Croakings of bullfrogs
gather like an ancient chorus
on this evening when that redorange eye

blinkless, peerless, storms

in an almost unmuttered memory
through bones of surging antique blood.

Lights from homes starlight
        the lake top as bass rise
and fireflies brighten
as though in a last torment
· before they vanish black
        into the night sounds
of dozing docks
creaking gently, sawing
like all these turning lives
into pink streaks of morning.

This night, this sonata
of light, enlists its own shadows
        that encircle its meaning,
and takes on prehistoric shapes
before outflanking dawn.

Should You Ask Me

The journey does not end here.
Around the bend, there's another.
Take your wounds and dress them
in the universal tongue.

Tendrils hang down from terraces
where stars sail past human memory
to where there is
no death, no tears, no war—
only paradise in the making,
making a rare appearance
for the discerning eye.

Here Lies Pocahontas

Here she lies, a princess whose memory is
    As sacred as Oregon's Mount Mazama,
A cross between village and temple,
    Preserved as a memory range
Between domains of the Powhatan Confederacy
    And her marriage to John Rolfe.
Two hemispheres united in a brief bio
    Who united mountains of sun and rain
In a zone of silence descended into these bones.

    Could she have known how
Her seeding would make her the would-be exile
    And the morning glory of the motherland?

Bay Farm Island

Wind blows windsurfers' sails seaward
beneath the full curve of a gull's wing.
Sand responds not to the steadiness of wind.
but just lies there, daring it to blow everything away.
as the wind tugs, ripples, vies with tides, surf.
and headwinds that turn tables
bent by seasons in the past.
Joggers oil their hearts with sweat,
prepare for races to be won nose by toe.
Voices of fishermen are caught and
fanned into the wind. Sleek hulls sail
into currents too loud for metal detectors,
too short for memory, too violent
for peaceful bicyclers on a Sunday afternoon.

Today

Today I can think of nothing to say.
Just listening to mute slivers of grass

As pink blossoms sputter around the path.
Fields of sunbright mustard throb in the day's
Distance, hawk-drifting with a bluish haze.
Today I carry with me a new cast
Of the French Revolution and at last
Will trust humankind, follow freedom's sway.
Today I see what risk it is to seek
Wisdom past understanding, to listen
To blind hawks, prefer the Han to the Ch'in
Dynasty, Athens to Sparta, to see
In nothing that nothing stays, and hasten
To leave unsaid for today "time to live."

Blood Feud

Often among relatives
are fought the fiercest wars:
Another Marduk
squares off against another Tiamat.
There rivalry,
hatred,
anger and betrayal
balloon,
peace vaporizes,
revenge beheads.

Everyone grasps
their imperial truth
and tears it apart in the name
of *the* truth.

No one is content
with relative truths.

Truth may be the last to be
disclosed
in the reckonings of destiny.

Warped self-understandings
pock mark history.
Misperception recycles
through the house of each
caught up
in sometimes fatal misjudgments
when drugged viruses are seldom the last.

Fear of uncertainty
and insignificance fuel
the quest for *the* only truth
so not everyone can be in the game,
in the same mindscape.

Abel slays Cain.
Brother slanders sister.
Thugs murder
for market shares.
Your God against our gods.

Weltschmertz settles in
like a yellow-diced fog.

In such a web, like a
a two-headed poisonous snake
there remains only contempt
for the joyous,
there remains only contempt
for community,
for the still point of our common humanity.

The Lotus Eaters

While Odysseus' love compels the returning blood
We sailors are home from our wanderings.
No more sail-shaped wails or blasts of fevers for us.

We celebrate no more rowing with him,
No more laboring in that wind-slammed sea,
Anchoring our muscles with a weary manliness.

Instead we gaze upward at seablue skies
That do not rainsquall work.
No more wanderings for our home is here.

After drinking from the lotus plant
We can set the stars on fire,
Melt summer's heat with ice,
Wed connoisseurs of symbolic dreams,
And, though lethargic, while
Propped beside beds of flowers
We listen to steadfast streams,
Not in a frenzy of the half-waking life,
But in swallows of pacific bliss
On sheets of forgetfulness
In the land of the Lotus Eaters.

over white corn, plump tomatoes
my sister bends
in the center: the sun

Double Shot
for Rita
This stillness buzzes, dear,
with light years in the morning's
solitude across avocado-toned fields.

Rivulets of snow resemble
the shape of your arms open
across the face of a jade-green mountain
shrouded in purple and blue haze.

In this our early rising
pine cones shadow limber limbs,

lumbered with seeds.

Even grasses, sweet now with those aromas
of the wild, are caught
in this dancing energy
unthought in
weathered elixirs,
sorrel bridles of the moon.

Sun-forgotten valleys too
(and we've embraced a few)
take their place in interstellar space,
assume complexions ever possible in a face.

Myron's Discobolus
(the *Discus Thrower* by the 5th century B.C.E. Athenian sculptor)

All this time he has sweated
For each day's release,
Each hour's ache, his muscles ideally poised;
He dreams one day he will launch it into the sun.

With a faint smile, he muses about that.

Curling fingers over the discus edge,
He takes a stance, knees bent, rotates back and forth
In a half-circle until he comes full circle.

Like a dervish, he spins and lets flow
Past horizons past, art transcending art.

The discus arches through a pastel sky,
And a little sadly returns to earth
To lines measured more than once.

Times and time again he rotates,
Spins into a white heat,

Blurs in whirl after searing whirl
And releases.
Spinning and throwing,
With his gasps a melodic repose,
He still believes he can reach the sun.

Still Life Still Moving

Quietude this morning halts as
quail scoot into
the underbrush.

A sentinel jay screeches,
cleaves the air.
Day is underway.

Snow still lines the purple mountain
that looks so still,
preserves a postcard

life so still we call it still life—
until we get closer,
stalk the path of

vibrations in the mysticism of granite.
Undetected motion
is what we call

permanence.
Even the music we assume is
dead wood,

feeling tone in another form,
undulates
in memory and transition.

Still this stillness buzzes
alive with light.
Soon the children of yesterday

will begin again
throwing a stick to a black Labrador
who jumps into a mountain ·

stream and
does not tire
of retrieving the stick

then shaking off
water that soaks his fur.
Isn't it true that day

is always
underway
even at midnight?

Novice Mind

Nothing here except the wind,
the wind in the pines,
wind's sound on the sound of water
the sound of wind in the mind.

No one here in this solitude
except that hawk circling the khaki hills
within hay-colored streaks beneath
immaculate blue sky.

No one here
except the novice mind
next to minnows that dart and dance
along the shore.

Novice mind: make a note of that:
the journey mirrored in a thousand
solitudes when you realize the inescapable
love of fate does not always define you.

In the Mountains of Southern Oregon

With their different layers of shade,
the mountains of southern Oregon
tuck behind one another in the orphic light.

Pointed treetops puncture foothills,
cut into a graying base,
suggesting how small the houses are.

A flotilla of golf maintenance cars
trim the fairways, making them more fair?

A grassy odor tingles the air.

Horseshoe pit shows wrinkles from last night's match
between codgers and young bloods.

Day lilies so still, hold their breath.
Distance in a bluish haze
offers an airy summons to enchantments that reveal
what uncreated heavens await.

The Odor of Spearmint

The odor of fresh-mown spearmint
is brief yet lingers on the air,
compels awareness if not acknowledgement,
of a slice, an angle of approach,
a truth outside this skin,
a survivor that drips over the latest definition,
the flesh that sums up another light within us.

Meditation at Muir Beach

Dunes in miniature wrinkle
the beach's lip as steady winds
whip the sand into beige
ribbed brows.

Whitecaps flare in rhythm;
surf tumbles into galloping
piano fingers.

A lonely gull tames her shyness;
her head tilts inquisitively
as she searches the beach.

Hers is a hunger.

Mine is how to stitch scar tissue,
another crackling of the heart,
one of love's crueler days.

Out there a hospital ship
drones seaward, its funnels
eclipse into fog. It can't
do a thing about these
drops that slowly wind
their way down my body
and color the sand redwine.

But there is in these wild waves
a peace between memories.
I can forget. I have before;
once memory and regret have
buried me in two.

After awhile the bleeding stops
as do the calls, and

like the gull, I shall fly
down the beach
and roll back out to sea.

Setting Sail

With energy that matches uneven mountains,
I climb into the boat,
Feel spindrift across my face and set sail,
Navigate this expanding channel
And head for the open sea.

For awhile the fog enshrouds
Then begins to lift and
At last burns off, exposing
Discernible latitudes of compassion.

Finally free from plumb lines and
No longer tempted by love or hate,
I am born once again
In each awakening of the sun.

At sea I embrace the wave-slitting
Fairness of the boat
And no longer touch the leaves of yesterday
And no longer bleed the leaves of yesteryear.

cows chew on
one side then the other
whitecaps through the fog

We Who Refuse to Die

Do not salute you and your private
Grievances shot up into public tragedy.

Domestic snipings, a vested interest in war,

Expressed as militant purity, your ideology's

A pretext for a new world order of old betrayals.
In your delusions, you continue to believe

Your hatred is the only true religion
And a cure-all for the body politic.

In your delusions, you believe your brand
Of politics that crushes human freedom

And destroys individual vision, is the only one.
You are the "true believers," recyclers of old grievances,

Trained by regimented bigots and
Committed to a rationalized collective delusion.

At the County Landfill

Gulls circle, attack, light, circle in swirls,
wing spreads menacing some things edible
beneath used garbage can lids, picnic baskets,
in the refuse of this wasteland.

The gulls do not circle the
mounds covered by black tarpaulins where
wood slat weights and chopped tires hold down
garbage in the face of northeasterly gusts.

Nor do gulls circle above
black puffs from bulldozers that burst
in pipe smoke puffs, adrift in the breeze.

Instead, the gulls swoop to snatch at food beneath
wine barrels broken and bread baskets,
recycled forms, anemone petals sun-dried,
brooms with no memories,

spotted sofas, flower pot shards,
arts of the discarded, spineless chairs,
and rain soaked planks, all
gulping the sun before being plowed under.

Lives invested in usefulness,
bent bird cages, shelf lives,
shapes of hidden biographies,
transmigrations, western skies
fine-tuning old songs of the east.

They are all here:
coming to terms with time's
prints, in tire treads,
ghosts that outlived their usefulness
in the use of being seriously taken.

When My Heart Print Bleeds

In sprays of morning my heart print bleeds red
With flint-chipped flames
For your voice breathes a sultry sonnet sound,
Your touch lures me beyond imprints of clay.

Your eyes draw kisses in blue lights
Of thighs that expose this yen's arc,
Those suns that rise along your finger tips
Nestling gently on yellowy sun-strobed waters.

This our dance, in honey-thirsting winds,
Revives all life from graves long lonely
With a grace unplanned as though
In a defiant fist of greener leaves, bursts us free.

Viva La Vida
(words at the bottom of Kahlo's *Still Life*, a portrait of watermelons)
for Frida Kahlo

You estranged hawk-browed seared angel:
how many agonies could you bear
in forty-seven winters?

All the ripe watermelons in the world,
blood red with symbolism, seedy,
loves that ran through hips of yin,
monkeys of yang, could not brush off
brushes with death or the arrows
of St. Anthony, you deer wounded
by hubby Diego's betrayals, as lover and son,
pigments of the subconscious
that animated your portraits, your ash-smeared passions,
for once in a frame, you gave birth to your self.

You finally came home to old Mexico,
to the dream textures your realities stroked everywhere,
to the self-divided colors of your heart and hearts
taken up in red, orange, and yellow flowers in your hair,
in the revolutions of your obsessive demons.

From the history of this wrist
for Athena

From the history of this wrist
to the mystery
of a madsong stanza
dust runs after India ink.

We do not have to human skull
drum ourselves into the void.
This blue blue dream of you
glides over hamlets yet unnamed.

244

You lure us on to discover
the furies as well as holy ones
are pervaded by luminous
metaphors and skies that laugh.

No, the dream of you is not over:
you kindle in our hearts
unperceived lightning
that fields those infinite questions.

High in the Sierras

Granite
    awaits to
    be reshaped from unpolished drifts, eggs,
        boulders' primeval in up-
        heaval bursts now droned, drummed like

Lake
    reflections
    that jitterbug off untimed birch limbs
        lightning strobed with eyes closed,
        shapes music as dove-thought smoke wafts.

Wild
    berries from
    antediluvian snow-crests issue
        sorrel in dried cusps, in streams
        of despairing joy unbloomed.

Pine
    needles reel,
    sundance the wintriest ends of snow
        a resolution that
        foreshadows another name.

Trout
  sense minnows
  hide in green-blue shallows, bait for flies,
    cruise murky brownish beds
    pause to hang in currents like lead.

Here
  the circle
  remains to be broken, to cast to-
    morrow to hungry fish,
    to allow snow to form and fall.

Retouching

What would you give to relive days when tadpoles
swim in a cup as you shuffle home in wet galoshes
after the school bus is gone over the hill?

Or to hear bullfrog choirs in the fishpond
suddenly become quiet in front of a raccoon
whose cunning lights up the koi-scented night?
What would you give to mount your stallion
and hear the saddle squeak
as you swing your youth up and over?

Or to see your father's face
as he cuts predawn ears of corn
before the sugar returns down the stalk?

What could you give?

All That is the Case

Many embrace the dogma of this natural world alone:
no archangels, no leprechauns, no daemons, no divine.

We have our methods, bombs, our paradises lost:

we grunt, groan, and sometimes miscalculate.

The layers of our ignorance dissolve as we are
slowly exposed to eyelids of galaxies upon galaxies.

We discover numinous reverence
that breathes in a mummy.

Then we probe the unconscious as the way
to overcome flowers hammered into stone.

· We soak in the notes of numbers and intuit ten,
the perfect number for an odyssey beyond the beyond.

We relearn to touch the nail on our little finger
as the first light of rare extraplanetary wavelets.

Then can we savor the beach at Ipanema
when we taste lemons buoyant with solitude.

The Promenade

You have come to promenade
and not just in the way one moves in the fox trot
but in a time that is not just linear
for there is always a cosmic sway.

That is no exaggeration:
the bored and thirsty take exaggerations as true
since they cannot seem to find the lemon
beneath the shade of yellow,
perhaps because they are dying
bound to craving or maybe filled-in pauses,
simulated conversations.

Promenade as yourself for
there are dragons in climbing out of yourself,

quarks in your soup:
yet being-yourself-boundaries
which are practically helpful
are ultimately false.

You can open yourself and espouse the heavens.

Serenity

I wander through
 a deep green field
and sit   beside
a gurgling   brook
and open   a book
of poems:

Sultry in the leaping
sun,
their syllables
                       color unresolved
confessions,
that make me
               want to drift
under cemetery trees.
They course through
             a percussion of syntax,
a range   of unborn dreams,
griefs that break down   into vibrations.

Such currents   listen to
the roots of my aging
domains   of fire-storms,
reeds that hum violins.

Occasionally I look
away
               from these lines

and note   resurrection
plants
spy clumps   of bunchgrass,
pockets of goatsbeards
and bluebells
                  from the motherland,
and tune in   to coiled vistas of exile.

The sun's dyings   make leaps
that tease
                  and awaken my ears
to prehistoric ferns.
Butterflies hip hop peninsulas,
rocks waltz,   wind rumbas
through the grasses,
wisdom   flows with the currents
out of fires and demons   as they pass

At the Café Intermezzo
(after looking through Wittgenstein's *Tractatus*)

It was as though we were released
from a long wait, in lines
steeped with extraplanetary summers.

No longer were we entranced
by games using language
pretending to reflect states of mind
or to reflect split seconds
between boredom and a divided self.

In a round about way, we discovered
something unforeseen: not just to hear
echoes but how to see them,
not just to say "the Big Dipper rises"
but how to know as well as say
"the Big Dipper *breathes* as it rises"

249

when the day's wind
began to sweep us clean
with alternate perspectives
as our eyes were dilated with insight.

Thereafter's Hand

There is no faith without separation. —Paul Tillich

Separate from you
I can see now
how it was necessary
for me to be able to say anything
about us at all
such as "I" and "thou."

How close we were
in our connections to aboriginal shores,
the navel of our home.

We discovered how closeness
evaporated as we entertained
the being of light
where your body
symbolized our unshared grooves.

Yes, separation has its
boundaries that entwine
with necessities just as ivy curves
around a trellis,
just as sound enjoys
a pause in each silent syllable.

When the Sun Dances

Red is the habit
of eating or eaten.

Ash the cradle
of war and worm-eaten.

Blush is the laughter
of rolling down dunes.

Brown be the mind
of deepest stone hewn.

Black is the accent
of kimonos of light.

Jade the newborn
of charms at their height.

Blue is the cadence
of night birds that dance.

While bone is the body
of fertility chants.

Bringing in the Laundry

The clothes pulley forth on a bow-dyed line.
Limelight bleaches them.
They hang out in a primitive noon.

Their numbers bleed a starched passage.
Buttons unbuttoned reveal a nation of arms.
My landlady arrives in a pink limousine.

She contends the primitive is a reappearing art,
Pulls out a naked gun and stakes out
The will's mesmerizing gulag getaways.

This Prison

An encrusted soul in this matter's visitors hour,
I tell the truth in lies,
at times, cultivate laughter,
stitch exile deep into dawn,
and never try to untune
the contrapuntal sabbaths
between thrash and rhapsody.

Yet, in prison, I am told what to do,
eat slop, urge justice to remember
justice, watch chickens scratch the earth and
peck for corn whether it be a Tuesday
or time lost in the tides of forgetting.

Each day I treasure my broken capacity
to survive another beating,
another humiliation, another death march
by wolves hungry for another mind
to drug, another spleen to rip out.

I survive by a primal melody within.
When I suggest *nothingness,* it responds
with *love.* If I murmur *death,* it counters
across the gap with *freedom.*

Deer Tracks in the Snow

Deer tracks in the snow:
The deer are worthy of reverence.
They might just outlast greed
And haphazard ignorance.

Eagles nest in two mountain trees:
They invite admiration.
Whether they survive their daily

Death sentences is an open question.

The *David* and *Pietà* by Michelangelo:
Their fortitude and spirit are prized.
Perhaps these may be ways of
Dealing with our usual nemeses.

Traces of the divine here and now:
Can the divine in us outgrow
Abuses by the religion of politics and wars
That terrorize this sacred earth?

To Kiss the Earth Again

Untie that mind
reasoned to the death
above thighs of earth's last moon.

Clear the debris
of intimate scalpels
and live the music unconquered.

Untie that body
and let ardor rip
tangs of the smoking sun.

For a Laughing Philosopher

Levity is your wisdom's signature.
You do not speak in straight forward answers.
Instead, you juggle with words
that become seventh generation sagas
exploring paradoxes
in mindscapes of memory.
Like a mirror dipped in ticking waves
you reflect the many angles of love.
That is why you bring such joy

253

to the dance, why
your temples of sunshine
rouse the flesh to over and under,
why we discover
summers in the ice, and
like dancers of vision, color
the unconscious shapes of the eye.

A Bee's Blossom to Bloom

A bee ferries
from blossom to bloom
in meadows
penciled with sunlight.
She buzzes
in catechisms of valleys
that match
matchless insomnia.

Like earrings
once thought lost in the rain,
such a body
marries sacred awe
with the odor
of peach blossoms
as she rides
blooms to blossom.

The Sandpipers at Coronado Beach

An oil tanker remains unmoved,
so far without a spill,
near the end
of the age of oil.

A company of sandpipers
work their bills into the sand

while keeping a lookout,
tiptoeing like kids wearing spiked heels.

Gulls eye what the sandpipers have found,
ever ready to steal away
an unguarded morsel.

Centuries of waves
wash up fish and mollusks,
luring and feeding the birds
until two children run after them.

The birds hurry
until their legs blur into flight
as they swing their way
up the beach.

Two men jog by
as a helicopter whirls out to sea
to islands beyond the beyond.

The birds return
begin feeding again,
ever vigilant, seeking
to avoid a telltale ambush.

I Want to Remember

for Rita

I want to remember
your skin
that breathes

your silence
embracing the sea

your smile
a memory of home
your love

a first light of rare beauty
that lifts art
beyond readings of the blood
in windworn stones.

Castanets

Castanets
click an incantation
beyond the paths of philosophy
where questions
of self-overcoming
no longer puzzle the mind.

Castanets
clap for an incarnation
within the dance of philosophy
where daylight promotes
history as bleached thigh bones in
sand dunes marked by cycles of hunger.

Castanets
click an invocation to peace
past the scents of philosophy
to deepen the astrophysics
of the formerly unwritten page
aglow with undressed metaphors.

Castanets
clap as couples dance the fandango
with avatars of philosophy
as guitars of galaxies shimmer
where the unconscious unveils
ecstasies that rise from the whys of dreams.

Going to the Well

I go to the well for water
for that is where there is rope
bent with meaning as scene-drenched
as mountains beside the sea.

I go to the well to forget
the image that appears there
tucked between intertexts
with their heart lines of bittersweet tales.

I go to the well to wet my hair
torched with dreams in nightmare forests
with their deafening midnight pulleys
that stretch recollection into philosophy.

I go to the well to rediscover
what I can remember
about you as a swarm of rhythms,
a pond as natural as a pause between circles.

I go to the well to uncover new moons
behind every other sail
and still dance unrivalled
on quilts of violins and bassoons.

I go to the well to shake the hands
of insomnia where mediums say
my summers could be only sand
amid the shooting stars of blood.

I go to the well to watch stirring silence
outfox the drivers of anger who cannot
fathom how music's special weather
sounds seashells in cities beneath the sea.

Twilight

Light from the dying sun
clings to the yellow oats and antelope-green alfalfa.

Cows pause their chewing,
stare with salt-licked curiosity beneath a faint moon rising.

Sadness, blunt-throated, slouches at the supper table
as the man notes the valley verdant in its muteness.

Two horses, a buckskin and a paint, graze steadily,
and, on occasion, survey the purple-streaked slopes,

That sonata of bones running through
splayed lavender moments, dipping red.

A blue flower conjures extra-sensory life
amid the hay-mellowed hills beneath sketches of pink clouds.

Long silent bridesmaid, a white adobe chapel
voices adoration of the last and first God.

A red-tailed hawk reads a field with its tufts of sleeping
lovers as a hare listens, motionless. Dreams evoke the blues,
that ancestral hue, where angels alight on the prongs of repose.

Ode to Numbers

In mapping the rhythm
of tides,
while discerning
Pythagorean notes
in the forests of number,
these can be
counted on:
passages and

not the least paradoxes
with motions in mind,
equinoxes
that await
revolutions,
solstices
that orchestrate
returns.
Storms intrude
as though by design
as clouds, as elemental dust,
each stroke's theology
of the natural world.

Over and down, up and around,
numbers keep us
ordered with insight:
we listen to
storms of the sun,
heliotropes in love with peace,
rocks split
to find water,
blue-dream personalities
that shadow
falcons silhouetted against
dozens of moons.

Here we adore zeroes,
cardinals with celestial sails
and try to fathom
wounds of the solar system
that make us into war lovers.
We note calculus in the music of things
and gather in magnitudes
of the heart
carnations
in seawater atmospheres.

The Open Doors

I open the door to ravines of laughter.
The wind bangs it shut.

Again I open the door,
this time to deny the literalism of history.

The storm slams it shut,
unhinges those revisions of our love.

Again I open the door,
voices eclipse silence in the coin of words.

I open the door again.
To my surprise, your open yours.

We begin to see forever,
taste infinity of the sun's eroding hush.

This Venture to the Woods

Spontaneous this going, this discovering
swooping birds that draw double helixes
as if crimsoned out of a dream montage.

April clouds slowly emerge
slowly from nowhere, blue boardwalks,
beds of guitars, strings of lupines.

A gurgling stream scales slopes of a hill
while an abiding hamlet continues
to erode from the flurry of cities.
Along with its levitation of leaves, the wind
sands the country church's vital massage
in a steeple of settings.

Far off, beyond a cloud cover's sail
the sun's shadow boxes through
magnetisms of moons, connects us.

Day descends on a swing of ticking,
blanketing into dusk
water lilies of unrivalled reflections.

Looking for Home

Stone idols are simply stone,
unripe cocktails,
a surface rubbing
in shadows of sky.

Yet inside history
we long
to be in our home again.

Our lost innocence
tries to recover itself
in the flows
of soothing silence,
dreams of the timeless,
and in our music's
untamed country of bones.

Our lost innocence
tries to recover itself
in memories after midnight,
in dappled gatherings of moonlight,
and in that rare yoke of lost wisdoms.

Early the Late Sun Rises

When it is too late, you discover how early
the late sun rises
and all along your bags,

bows and arrows,
are not packed, ready to go.

How brown and brown
green earth's green becomes,
how time swallows
circles of voices we once knew,

Who weaved in and out
of our generation
biographies of everyday,
former addresses presently
resolved in mists, now seen
with a kind of clarity.

When it is too late, you discover
how early
the late sun rises.

When Time Warps Time

Weeks, eras, and days uncover eggshell threads
that connect us through dust, dreams and galaxies;

Epochs then seconds weave tangerine threads
that link our vibrations rising from winds and wood;

Time out of mind as well as weeks point to cobalt threads
that join us as tanagers and kestrels of the spirit;

Fortnights then nanoseconds discern strawberry threads
that fuse us with lips of ginger and thyme;

Hours alongside sidereal days venture sea green threads
that unite us with piccolo notes that do not fade;

Dated moments and years unveil orchid threads
that play our fingers on all-too-silent drums;

In a wink, hereafters then hours recount coral threads
that blend us as we open with open hearts;

Untimely moments and weeks find marigold threads
that fill us with secrets running from nowhere;

Microseconds and leap years speak umber threads
like shorebirds flying beyond the erosion of memory.

Slowly

for Rita

Slowly history tingles my hands like crested dunes,
slowly delightful silences hit me when I sense primitive hunger,
slowly in the corridors of recollection, labyrinths hide me,
slowly I hate my poems, toss them to the northern and western winds,
slowly these bones glide past a flame into midnight seashells,
slowly down the garden path, I follow the mistress of sleepwalkers,
slowly on this afternoon, my body is exhumed by driven nets,
slowly docile boardwalks double in peninsulas of fog,
slowly philosophy delights in nectars of the moon,
slowly I do not know the differences between night and day,
slowly a meadow inside teases me into gulfs of sunlight, while
this love for you swells and swells that madness in the music I wear.

A Close Shave

Lather his face, I told him.
He shaved my father's weathered face
with the scent
of brush-stirred soap
in his remaining afternoons.

The razor sounded like ripped sheets
as it cut his whiskers
at their graying roots,
followed the contours of his face
in a thinly-bubbled swath.

Each stroke shaved away the stages
of days and weeks
beneath his word-tried lips,
along his jaw's lines,
below his sideburns.

Time, he knew, grows back,
covering our lips, resisting
the smooth, the shaven
in favor of a blade that cuts us clean,
leaving the rest to bones.

Moving On

You keep
looking for ways out of your history,
afraid of your face becoming a wrinkled boot,
your bones no longer cunning traces of the blood.

You want
to forget your hunter origins
blue-green foam in waves of mothers, and
deny who you are, where you come from.

You hope
to rise into a spirit, ascend
into the heavens to forget who you are.

You have
no quarrel with chimeras, may parade
a lion's head around a goat's body
to deny what generation you are.

You still
are enfleshed, boxed memories
taped into their darkness, longing
ever longing to leave with a new address.

Bus Station at the Border

A woman, wearing a pale T-shirt which reads:
"I _____ and,_____on the first date," sleeps next to her purse;
Beneath a sign that reads: "Will not work for anything"
the merchant watches over his store of fake silver;
In a moment of fantasy, one astronomer strings
together black holes with anti-matter
as another pilgrim waits while reading the *Bhagavad-Gita*;
A mother tries to escape her demons.

A tour bus from a city unknown pulls into the station.

Suddenly the woman wakes up and grabs her purse.
A divine marks the mystical as the mother of actual occasions.
The aging bodhisattva with windworn hands
unravels a map of Galilee and points to the sea.
Another physician who doctors the soul invites the miraculous.

Ready to embark, the clown makes sure his smile does not droop
while a math teacher dons spectacles made of equations.
A statue smiles as it listens to the dead whispering
as the mother fumbles but does not forget her beads.

From the bus, more tourists debark in islands of sunlight.

One Avenue of Dreams

Dreams that allow
the unmeasurable
can be realized
without rigidity or rejection's slip.

Though silent, you can catch moonlight
off homeward leaves
and the scent of wild plums
on Saturday night recollections
where the heart
mythologizes
the reveries of imaginable space
and where the cratered moon,
without inhibition's blush,
nightly caresses the cheek of Endymion.

A Foggy Morning

and no life to go to.

You can barely see the river.
The fog invites you into hiding.

Touch heard alone seems to recall
the nexus with any world.

Like Dante, you can get lost,
a midlife crisis.

You can sleep with doctors of desire
and refuse to be.

You can miss the force of blood
in the autumn rose.

And unmilk the soul in
unleavened valleys of the dead.

Then there's no life at all
save the restive returns

of unbelieving fire.

In the mirror there is stillness;
it is only noon.

Two Gulls at Goat Rock Beach

A gull eyes the party talking and laughing
as they eat taco chips, hot dogs, and cookies.
Her teenage son pecks at her breast
whining with impatience.

Unflappable, she keeps her eye out for a morsel
dropped or carelessly tossed away.

The gulls are veterans of human excess.

Her son continues to whine an alarming sound,
occasionally pecks her breast, even plucking feathers.

His mother continued to steady her gaze on a
bread crust or a chips bags left on a blanket
while the people gallop into the surf.

Her son continues to whine, impatient for attention,
maybe food, somewhere between another rite
of passage and a war chant.

Fort Ross at Midsummer
[Czarist Russia's trading settlement
(1812-1841) on the northern California coast]

Perched on tree limbs, egrets sound low in threesomes.
The fort basks in a mellow mid-afternoon.
A calm sea calms even as it dashes
the rocks, rocking a seal into her new position.
In the distance a fishing boat sways
as poles fish on port and starboard sides.
An eggshell streak of fog lies on the surface
of the blue foam-whipped sea.
In mild sea breezes and above swells of kelp beds
eucalyptus leaves waft down,
spinning like sardines above the sorrel bluffs.

Today blood and breath focus on a tall strand of oats.
Orchid hues jostle with sea green auroras of the wild rose.
Here too love continues it meandering course
while the spirit spreads sunflowers down and up the coast.

> **spring blossoms**
> white puffs
> roll across the roadway

> **Zen Sight**

> 1.

To be the sound of water
is to be between
the sound of white
and whitewater.
No longer to need
to rhapsodize or canonize
the eschatology
of summer trees.

2.

A certain joy shapes
our loneliness
and finally fashions it.
A gateless gate: here
your thinkings crystalize.

3.

Rain beating down on the rain
on an old man in Tennessee:
a parrot cocks her head,
the river keeps flowing.
They all listen
as stars in the fall
fall asleep.

4.

A new way to spoon
eaten thoughts
into a pregnant emptiness:
here, step into this
picture of four pears
on top of a blue mountain,
yes, the one there with
a blue wren on a blue branch.

5.

The work of breeding dreams:
the circular skins of me
and me. How final, how free
the wild swans
in a bleeding twig's kingdom.

6.

By plum trees
the lovers lying
there. And the moon partly
hidden. All together their
lines, which you can barely
make out, map out a sacred space;
centered thus, they all share
the waterfall at dusk.

7.

Nothing exists. Here hangs
a metaphysical tale
on comedians in the dark.
Striking a blue match,
the muscular one plays
a mean jazz guitar
with a clear blue voice
of a sound clearing.

8.

Upon a sun-hammered hill
clusters of knotted oak
paint the true body.
Like trusted habits
shedding snakeskin,
the fallen leaf's
eternity
resexualizes.

9.

Amid parabolas
of soul

and skeins of memory,
a squirrel sits
motionless
as we pass.
Deepening, the river
swirls once again.

10.

As stars skate
across the pond,
a marigold motions
with this aside:
travel light, she says,
*if you wish to approach
the fathomless plum.*

11.

Answer to the riddle
of April rain:
brazened hawks encircle
yellowing flesh
made of yellowing flesh
made of the music of more.

Green

1.

In China, jade. And the taste of jade.

2.

Blues, yellows all green where Monet's lilies float.

3.

The horror of green is that it might know everything.
Remedy? let green ripen. mix its own colors.

4.

Green blends in time to cool and form the Chinese
character "Ai" where the heart is swept by the breath.

5.

Camouflage, elegant green in mindful aboriginal

6.

hiding. Green grow the elms along the familial stream.

7.

In the war of weeds, green's postlude follows its own
path to applause.

8.

Plato embraces green; Aristotle the measured.

9.

Green's pigment mirrors blue's sky, returns its hues
within the dissolution of time.

10.

Prophetic traits realize adversity is expensive; green's
darkest light creates anterior to truth alloyed.

11.

What is praised are the autobiographies of green,
hexagons of the dreaming self.

12.

History living draws anatomy's lesson; green's peace
is scaled by the heart. Red's yellow wars to be

13.

at war. "Surrender to your heart," sayeth the green
novel to the witching catacombs of allegory.

14.

Inevitable jealousy, though envy be green. A canvas
without borders that venerates anything hidden, green
confuses age and youth with the whole

15.

truth. Green postdates death as the scar the wound.

16.

Green's parents: blue's pink and yellow's red.
Grandchildren soar black into a spectrum of blue.

17.

Unlike the last of the last judgments, which tends to see
red, green rests, dons the shade.

18.

By reflex green bites, chooses denying time, with virtual

19.

endurable vision. Green senses sexual energy is the house
of blue, unrequited, that champagne of indecision.

20.

Green on the palette spreads the history of art. There is a
mystic undercurrent in the bluest of wills.

21.

Parents and child form at least three. Listen and form
a rainbow out of paths that fork from misfortune borne alone.

22.

Motionless, green hangs timeward, roars through grief
and those necessary valleys of brass.

23.

Striated muscle, one of green's former names, yields
to a wind of kisses, dances among the aspens.

24.

A witness to the future, green does not focus on failures.
It undresses only for the many.

25.

Green's symphony greens the empty hill, husbands energy
romancing the classical.

26.

Improvise green jazz do scat talk blow your horn
pound those keys blow baby blow keep smokin'

27.

Green does not put pressure on Once-In-A-While
but modulates the timbre of a symphonic garden.

28.

Cemetery lawns, green grow the rushes O-
ver mass graves and shooting parades.

29.

Violet and green: all the relatives in the world,
branches connecting life and form's ash-blond knowledge.

30.

When yellow is angry, green leans on the gravity of blue,
the joyous "living with despair" blue.

31.

A web of miracles, green embraces the sonata ear of this
hour, transcendental jazz, third eye of nowhere.

32.

Green snake eyes watch for progeny: yellow
games and blue true roads.

33.

Green tends to non-violence while undoing death's undone.

Ages of Rock

That rock all afternoon
shows nothing but shifting sunlight

Yet that passiveness
reveals a wisdom akin to silence.

Soccer Teams
(Winters, California)

boys play on the lower field;
      upper field:
the girls jog their warm ups.

evening's sunlight
flies and gnats pluck—
still no summer ripples

summertime voices
splashes and reflections
a crow carries a nut

Dialectic of the Deep

Sand: | **Sea:**

Where do you come from o
sea that slaps the land?

From a trailing wind and sea
dreams of a wife of night.

And who is your mother o
sea of essential things?

A siege of mutual
love, naked as now, who
refuses none.

What do you chart with your
olive eyes o main of the
north country?

Ashes of butterflies
who stirrup like the
phoenix.

And who be your father o
wave of the south?

A stallion of those unmarried
appaloosa mornings
who bears a sailor's grief.

And where do you go
o sound of the riddled sea?

To that prehistoric
atlas with its salt
water tomorrows, its
eden of kingfishers.

Hawai'i Nei

Foam and waves
A moment's reef:
Luaus, leis, and mahalos;
Poems for palms,
Pearls for memories.

Unearthing: A Life Recollected by Cheyenne "Magic" Amenyana

Le jour est proche ô mes soeurs de grandeur
Où nous rirons des mots guerre et misère
Rien tiendra de ce qui fut douleur...
—Paul Éluard

Yo soy yo y mi circunstancia.
—José Ortega y Gasset

In all my days, I saw through the blurs of traffic,
        hawked visions for a living,
was a surveyor of the mind
        who cherished the love of freedom.

Among my adventures, I rode to India on an elephant
        stitched with mandarin butterflies;
I danced across the cosmos
        and searched the interiors of time

for the original atom,
        changed my name to Sleepwalker-by-Fascination,   *10*
and mapped the angle of refraction
        in an orchestra of silence.

On zany nights I strolled amid radio waves
        reading Boethius' *Consolation of Philosophy,*
Murasaki's novel *The Tale of Genji,* and Meister
        Eckhart's sermon "God Laughs and Plays";

revered enchanted sleepers and noted
        snowy owls within a sand painting,
came upon vigils to the evening star,
        a spectrum of light in which to say yes,   *20*

whose dimensions inspired masters of divinity
        to ponder and make manifest the soul,
and presumed a cosmic sunrise
        in the chronicles of conquest.

I discerned a life
        expectancy that included string vibrations
passing through the dimensions of earth, wind, fire,
        water and the practice of non-violence,

unearthed hymns of the everlasting
        in interstellar space and   *30*
yearned to smolder and burn
        like the poems of Rumi in fields of love.

In my time here I endured hatred, ignorance,
      terror and genocide,
became a casualty in war,
      a philosopher in peace,

mixed dates with puddings,
      plums, and fairy tales
and conducted foreign affairs
      in the poetic vernacular.   *40*

It was my imagination that built an acropolis
      in the sumptuous northwest
while searching for love after love
      in the dark comedy of manners

only to uncover untapped
      symphonies of biorhythms and
scared flying squirrels with
      the electric charms of unnamed anarchists,

intensely lived my soul as though love is the whole
      and did not mortgage my days;   *50*
who with my family went
      canoeing long into dusk and

underwent sessions in meaning therapy
      to translate the primal scream:
who heard within flights
      of swans the company of Christ.

reforested pines and firs across continents
      for the sake of the wild in wilderness:
who trolled poetry for a second self
      and reeled in a lonely muse.   *60*

drew a map of faceless wrinkles
        as an index to the origin of the universe
in the Big Bang and danced white-hot with
        tambourines into shades of the Hindu god Shiva,

welcomed smells of unbridled horses
        in the rosemary of forget-me-nots
when expanses of sand
        opened the mind with subterranean sutras;

assumed modes of the enshrined and
        drummed labyrinths of the beatific vision   *70*
while speaking Gaelic
        among the rhododendrons and tiger swallowtails;

who made ecstasy
        visible to the naked proposition
yet celebrated color dispersions
        playing pizzicato with the goddess of the present,

who greeted revolution
        with "to your health!," kicks of kung fu,
and regret, yet revived humanity
        with a toast to the inherent dignity of process;   *80*

whose slide trombones and kettledrums shimmered
        waves throughout the Milky Way,
cantered toward true justice
        with an eye toward the wisdom of the sages

mapped and studied genes before the advent
        of love-lies-bleeding flower beds,
doffed my aloha shirt while listening
        to the Tao of the Russian River with its soft jazz

scorned propaganda sporting thinly knit
    accents working as both a stonemason and cellist,   *90*
chanticleered Zen and the art of meditation instead of
    dispersing demonic thermonuclear brew across the world

tossed my salad days with tuning forks
    shaped by weathervanes and
sprayed stone cold tin pan hearts
    with furlongs of laughing gas

defused Ragnarok with olive, tea leaves,
    sage, and lotus petals;
and, in a moment of forgetfulness, simmered peppers
    until they favored false diamonds;   *100*

measured mountains moving
    by the returns of civil disobedience
and trained the will to power
    to reverence the mistress of destinies,

who grounded weapons of mega-deaths
    into plowshares,
practiced listening to survivors
    surviving as petroglyph ancestors

explored windworn and seaworthy atlases
    until I found terra incognita   *110*
and later rejoiced in sunsets
    as though they were seven kisses from holy women;

forgave the jaws of mood swings due to the varying
    frequencies of sound both far and near
and tangoed with zombies and salty dogs
    off the coast of Barbados

who scaled the libidinal process
        into a redorange nirvana
while bassoons and flugelhorns jammed
        in a jazz that floated up the pyramids at Giza and Copàn *120*

stressed the harmonic structure
        of Chinese puzzles in battle fatigue.
and charted virtual Viking explorations into the land of
        antinuke Powhatans. Ojibwas and Cherokees:

sounded capriccios in unsigned
        signs and honored elephant
tusks and the remains of indigenous peoples
        while disclosing a single eye

scattered ashes to the separation
        of radiation from matter   *130*
and composed ribs from designs
        riddled with trust:

whose exploits soared past evergreen
        Middlesex townships and
above anthems in a manger
        that became heliocentric:

who lavished navigators with orchids
        beneath timeless waterfalls,
painted in a chiaroscuro technique
        playwrights on an upbeat track,   *140*

dramatically filmed the migratory life
        of snowflakes
and made war on battalions of bacteria
        and epochs of viruses;

who became admiral to a fleet
    that included kosher dinner wines
while composing scores to flowered pistils and treble clefs
    in time's gray eyes

whose fading once as an author outside a text
    resembled fads with unseasoned horizons   *150*
yet recovered just enough to record the eruption of volcanoes
    on the ocean floor without drowning

spent afternoons scuba diving again and re-read the philosopher
    · Wang Yang-Ming while preparing undersea cameras,
and sketched swallows in Capistrano
    to discern family timelines through native skylights;

who helped free the slaves
    from tyrannies over body and mind
and was despised by fanatics that preached
    hatred to their militant followers   *160*

instinctively knew catastrophes
    lie in the interior valleys of caste,
lionized passions within
    the many-toned rainbow and lived for bronzed beauty,

burst through streets in Katmandu
    shouting "Long live the peacemakers!"
and inched closer to God
    in the settlements of brotherhood

now watch a blackbird eat and eat
    a peach until it falls half-eaten   *170*
and am dying to be sprinkled
    with the enchantment of diverse waters...

Notes

The epigraphs: "The day is near o my sisters of grandeur
When we shall laugh at words like war and misery
And nothing shall remain of that which was grief..."
—Paul Éluard (1895-1952) (my translation)

"I am myself and my circumstances."
—José Ortega y Gasset (1883-1955)

Lines:

32—Rumi (1207-73) (Jalal al-Din Rumi): Sufi poet of Islam.

53—logotherapy: founded by Viktor Frankl (1905-1997), who I met in
1973, is a meaning therapy rooted in his death camp experience
with insights from Existentialism.

54—primal scream: a therapy to treat emotional problems by
encouraging patients to relive and express their traumatic
experiences.

70—beatific labyrinths: I associate the secular beatific vision with the
labyrinths in the fictions of Argentinean writer Jorge Luis
Borges (1899-1986).

76—pizzicato: a light plucking staccato sound played on a stringed
instrument.

78—kung fu: ancient Chinese art of self-defense.

88—Tao of the Russian River. In Taoism, Tao is the source of all.
Influenced by Russian presence at Fort Ross (1812-1841),
California's Russian River empties into the Pacific Ocean.

92—thermonuclear brew: the moral choice to use nuclear power to
destroy here is likened to drinking a demonic brew.

97—Ragnarok: In Norse myth, final destruction of the world in a battle between gods and giants.

108—petroglyph survivors: drawings on rock made by a prehistoric people.

115—zombies and salty dogs: a play on words for the kinds of characters the narrator has met as well as two kinds of drinks.

117—libidinal process: a term encompassing the sexual drives in human development.

120—pyramids at Giza and Copàn: the great Egyptian Pyramid at Giza. The pyramid at Copàn in Honduras is the site of an ancient Mayan city.

124—Native American tribes, historically including Pocahontas (c.1595-1617) of the Powhatans.

125—capriccios: an instrumental composition that does not adhere to rules for any specific musical form and is played with improvisation.

135—manger: refers to the infancy narrative of Jesus in the New Testament.

136—heliocentric: a sun-centered view of the universe, first hypothesized by Aristarchus of Samos (c.310-230 BCE), was later "rediscovered" by Copernicus.

139—chiaroscuro: technique among Italian Renaissance painters (such as Leonardo da Vinci) to strengthen the illusion of depth on a two dimensional surface.

149—author outside a text: refers to the centrality of the text and
  disappearance of the author as though a text exists in a vacuum
  for purposes of interpretation.

154—Wang Yang-Ming (1472-1529) developed an idealist
  interpretation of Confucianism.

155—Capistrano: a southern California city where swallows annually
  return to the old Spanish mission there.

161—Katmandu: capital of Nepal, not far from the frontier of India.

The Hunt

Spring comes early this year
Melting ice, swirling streams, you hear.

Hunters are gone, hunting the hunted
And often they are dear.

These/Hymns of woods, blossoms' use

These
Hymns of wood
Offer solace, blossoms' use
Where silence confesses
A wakened tenderness drawn by courage flexed.
Each holds more than thundering wails, homages to midnight's
Unreasoning riddles, those soundless
Plums that yield possibilities.
Now
Each hymn dusts remembrance to find a hill that is
Centuries of wisdom in laughter, tracing
Its contours with undying syllables, veiled joy, praise.
Here we dance through blue snow and dark's thunder
Now

Bodega Bay
(site of Alfred Hitchcock's film *The Birds*)

At this forenoon's low tide, the seaweed surfaces,
bent, flattened.
Streams of self-preservation by clams
jettison from holes in the mud.
Dug in, no tide can pull them out to sea.
Trying to survive, no seagulls find them.
But their fate changes as clam diggers show up with shovels.

Farther out, a brown pelican scans the water for fish,
gliding five or six inches above the waves.
Gulls halt in the air, their wings dancing
as though to imitate a hovering kestrel.

A black cormorant spreads her wings to dry; she
harbors a wary green eye toward the pelican and the gulls.

I note how some birds, by affinity or descent,
are related to reptiles.

Along the beach this late afternoon, hundreds
of shore birds eat in a sluicing frenzy.

Survival is in the air, even the water.
We cruise over to dinner, share a seafood platter
of fresh scallops, clams, oysters and shrimp.

After dinner, we remark how the shadow
of the sun dial's stick, as it is cast by the sun,
has lengthened, how the day's circle is almost complete.

We discuss Hitchcock's *The Birds*
as we listen to cormorants vying for a spot
clicking their guttural grunt chatter
and haunting us in the trees.

Mellow Beyond Recall

These islands they green by the sea
For they are lovers at the dawn of
The gods. They plunge deeper than
Waking pain. These are the genius
of bones, inventors of the final strophe.

These islands, august lovers in their
Friendship with the sun, all marry into galaxies.

They do not martyr the details of forgotten
Springs but trace past the wrecks deep
Down through the resurgent maps of bloom.
Mellow beyond recall, they
Enter the blue-greens of the sea
With its leviathan names.
The mind that sings the green of the sea,
Like a dancer whose profile becomes the sculptor
Of time, is a lover. Such a one dreams
The dream of endless duplication, who breaks into
Nakedness for a shore without motion.
Mellow beyond recall, these islands recover
Desire behind the sex of politics, the politics
Of mere appearances, the theater that seems evergreen.
"Only in many worlds" they chant "are we one.
And nothing less." *Viva le symbolisme!*
These lovers salvage the body
Where nothing yelps loudest in susceptible love.
We forget and in the bas-relief of our forgettings
Have to repeat those unremembered cargoes
Of pain. In remembrance springs redemption.

Mellow beyond recall, these islands color the
All as light, when ignorance is torn from their eyes
And yields a rainbow's birth, the primordial *fa*,
The face aflame, purer than

Any blank eye, in the last say of the rose.

The mind that conjures the green of the sea
With its gargantuan crosses of mourning, invites
Lovers who with compassion lay the yawn
Of quivering eyes on reflective glass
And behold
The art of light in luminous sheaths
Where nothing molds out of courage steeled
A lotus, serene voice of the pleromic man.

Dreaming Double: Composition Study for Just Jazz

> *Chi e costui sanze morte*
> *va per lo regno de la morte gente?*—Dante

Do I dream? Trees nestled   *love's searing fragments*
Clouds hang like sex   *yellow stamens//intelligent sun*

Trains rumble through narcissistic hands *guts in a seaweed text*
We are not only eaters   *copper suns*
                try the classic end   *wrenches beauty*

Lady in purple grips her   *incest's frozen souvenir*
about to be robbed   *winter senses*

                his price means zero   *slice a wavering dialect*
holding a private gun   *can cinch a sucker*

his pitch is coming   *she senses Modigliani*

        wearing an ass's head   *dreams bicker in the bereaved*

reading Mallarme's faun she dreams   *a doctorate in sleeping*
                                    gulls
of seducing a goddess   *revolutionary proverbs*

when her pistol's enfleshed   *voluptuousness*
        in the fierce afternoon   *the lonely clutch*

am I dreaming   *summer by spools*
         this train   *cravings wired to thunder*
night proves longest   *squid this raw*

A floating flower:
just one catches
this poem of earth.

Ten More Miles of Dirt Road

The vistas are stunning;
Hay-bleached hills bake in summer's heat.
Turns and twists in the road
on the way to the lake seem
like time leans into the timeless;
but that is only a mask;
actually, it is only another bend in gravity
of the earth's seeming stillness;
and if you think for one moment
these are only sketches of a paradigm
you are mistaken;
this is a shadow of a gliding mirror,
a reflection of another reflection;

Soon we will be there
and the fish will be biting for we know
a hover of trout survived another winter
before the snow plows came
as our breath
makes another string of memories;
our touch
the butterflies of late afternoon,
lilies of projected scents,
lasting solitudes in the treetops of our days,
the unconscious at work in the design

of our forgetting's birth,
journeys of our flesh,
a hotel intimation of our passings,
our prehistoric configurations
that startle us even now.

Late Summer, San Gregorio Beach

for Rita

Lines in my book of poems
describe sunflowers that survive
the falling sun in a willow green solitude.
I look up and see
tongues of sand that
curve along the sea line
from a wave-twinkling sea
into a lagoon past
a cabin made of driftwood
to shield against the steady wind.

Your murder mystery depicts
jury tampering and a judge who
covers up his time with his district attorney mistress.
You blow a kiss my way and look up
from your book: next to seaworn branches,
off-white fishbones and chunks of chipped logs
wisps of algae hug, slide, and bob
with the tide inflow along the shoreline.

The seventh poem speaks of flint and older lyrics
where all we have are memories of memories,
auroras and lunar eclipses. Looking up, there
are no breaks in the poetic rhythm here:
crowds of gulls congregate
in pockets of gray; they flinch, fake biting
other gulls, clean their feathers,
always eyeing humans across the lagoon
for their bread and tortilla chips.

Your book's plot line includes a hung jury
and a declared mistrial; the judge is off the hook.
You look up and take in the scene: we kiss
as the gulls fly off again in charcoal
formations, circling ever circling
in gray pelican-winged callings against
a saguaro-green horizon
dotted with fishing boats trying to net
yellow fish, tuna and lingcod.

Saline Solution

As masts gently sway,
reflections dance
off the hulls and unfurled sails of
docked sailboats,
resplendent in the sun,
that contain
a community below decks
you don't always see,
close to the tides,
engaged in repairs to
the nets of flags,
washed, sanded, painted,
being restored by the water.

The Complete Reverie

The complete reverie is the poetic one,
sails of imagination puffed like an adder.

Dreams may fashion us like sand dunes
with crested solitudes
or as shipwrecks
until cosmic consciousness appears.

Reverie is memory's
circular time-space
that marks the magnetism of motion,
the unfallen apple, the recollected dream space,
vibrations of the earth.

Battered by storms and seas
our horizons still hum
with those gypsy hands
that keep forever ticking.

Recognize the sacred in the profane
and we embrace the cosmos.

The complete reverie is the poetic one.

Wars of Love

You say you have been resurrected, now that you
have overcome me and you.

You say you have escaped the clutches
of the day of the dead

And are alive again now that you have realized
what a make-believe the ego is.

You have never liked matter and spirit. You only
like them as one and the same.

*

But it does not bother me if matter and spirit
are not one and the same.

You are like a bird caught by smoke from a
raging bonfire on the beach.

I could not know you if both of us have
overcome me and you.

We are in the same picture, asymmetrical survivors,
pearl oysters best gathered in silence.

> kelp ropes and seaweed
> the odor of saltwater—
> history in layers

For Josiah Royce
(American Philosopher, 1855-1916)

Did the folks around Grass Valley fully appreciate
your thinking art from Berkeley to Gottingen,
Hopkins and Harvard?

The essential direction of your existential questions?

You who thought we learn most about ourselves
from others? You who thought God the ultimate individual
who suffers when we do? No wonder you valued community,
the great community, loyalty's social infinite, where each
person is a kingdom of ends.

Still I wonder, as dust settles on the daring of thought,
did the folks around here really appreciate your thinking part?

Renunciations

> You chant beyond the world
> and incline to dwell in camps above the snow.
> Still at sea you listen for ripples of
> wheat and corn, the taste of summer's fruit.
> Last year we renounced companies
> with their domino beds of sick revenge.
> Have we not spoken of the dust that lights, the

newborn renunciation that embraces and frees?
Pour some more coffee, gentle one, we have some
darkening sides of absences to bridge.

Circles of Rings

They echo each other
these circles of tones,
forming rings that echo
in the ring of things,
like El Greco,
foretastes of unreasoning toys.
They hover over fields
flushed by human moods,
fireless moons, kisses bearing riddles.

They echo one another,
forming frescoes of rings,
circles that mingle umber with joy,
fruit glazed with winter, fates fallen,
scrub oak sunsets, gazes through the easel.

Secco echoes echo one another,
alternate horizons,
much like Boccaccio, raindrop notes,
caves and misty cowslips, forming a ring of circles,
invented lake tops,
globes leaning toward countdowns,
tulips of insomnia.

You and I, Love

You explore
And I dream
Of soft summer sun
In haystacks along the river.

I dream and dream
By tablespoons of the romantic sun
(Intensity's best in narrow slits)
Away from the protocols of public abuse.

You run and run.
I do too.
We run in sacred circles of summer's sun.

You explore
And I dream
The many and the one
Even when the sun's sun is winter's one.

Drawing the Line

is drawn between what appears

and what appears
to be where worms crawl into
yarns of autumn's sidelong sleep.

You can, if you wish
act the sage
whose roar saddles
your memories of what appears to be
rather than play the fool.

There, even when dawn wakes
as geese fly overhead
you watch your love
assume the mercy
of passing through corridors
that do not end.

Flowers peek through the splendor
of what appears to be until, after

twilight, after the owl of Minerva
has flown,
the line dissolves.

Reaching for the Visions of Wisdom

Reaching for the visions of wisdom
I color an image that dances there:
you as a swarm of rhythms
with love as natural as summer rain.

Reaching for the visions of wisdom
there are verbal nightmares
with their semantic confusions
that turn recollection into philosophy.

Reaching for the visions of wisdom
I hug a tribe of kitharas and cellos
that shape movements between us
beyond native swan songs.

Reaching the silence of wisdom
in the shimmering decor
finds you and I without borders,
quartz now melted into liquid poems.

Birth of a Star

So hard to be
born, sometimes messy,
not as clean as we would like.
Then the sense of being
divined into memories
tunneled by light.

One moment
tiny, almost dwarfish,
pushed about
by winds, vulnerable to disease,
predators, and cosmic
collisions shaping dream stuff.

Then in the speck
of space we are here,
we grow darker than deep,
nudge the gigantic
with rust color spiraling
appetites, uncover black holes
in the beauty of reason,
bring a period to an end
by retrospective commentaries,
breathe in deeply
auroras lying on our backs
on docks at the ends of summer.

We go back back, back, back
to a time before our birth
when galactic seas, restless with storms
and nuclear reactions,
show how wonder allows us
to kiss the dawn, to note
silhouettes muskrats make as they swim
through ponds and those
staccato hoots of owls at night.

There we find our connection
to the insides of stars,
where the present past recycles future supernova
eruptions into the fall and rise of newborns.

Voice Made of Dawn

for Rita

Your voice made of dawn
hints at that august presence
of a life lived-in-spite-of.

You emerge from sways of dreams,
from the paradox
that reality approaches dreams,
as you intimate a voice that,
being born so many times,
lingers not just in my mind
but in a bliss as seablue as the dawn.

The grass is green
The sky is blue.
Things empty as they are.

your childhood chasing butterflies

across a paisley field
in them you crown monarchs
of the living dead
and celebrate
the lions of daylight

you come alive
when you are alone
wrestling spites
of time (so intimately
you unearth this
fragile plot) well then
clench the scruff of sky and love!
with cantos of memory
that swell through foraged dreams

they become your playground
of drums and stars

your childhood chasing butterflies
when you find resurrections
in the sculpted past
and the whining of plum wind
down shell shade
wired with all tomorrows
to a clockwise tongue

chasing sounds of butterflies down
lends random
shapes to instant
joy and there
the holy blooms
of madness
yield diviner sense

this ancient rite is
where you
net a tree of wisdom
running suns
down a lizard's tongue
before the dark
begins to plow
the snoring grass

Silence Before Silence

At dawn   mists

the sound of drakes   looming upside among the tules

the sun   wheel of the sublimest notion.

In a tule fog   a cranium that remains

nameless

present and unaccounted for: the one

a valley named feminine

cabarets there incline

toward rumors of yang

What could be could be
waiting

does not deter the unimaginable:

memory vessels the oceanic before
the waters broke,   the beloved community

without a signature   on precocious stone

Lines draw   the eyelids when

heaven in an uncooked instant

reaches

the body's dignity   freedom

from mere equatorial sight

Galliard

Igniting the rapture
a dance of the first magnitude: that
star-born infusion of nothing
in five steps.

True to Form, True to Chaos

True to form and, pregnant with form,
chaos winds its way through jagged limestone hills and
finds us still diurnal creatures in love with night.

True to chaos, caravans find truth
in divine laughter from
children in the wild on mountain tops.

True to form, sonnets can
emerge from chaos and plot their shapes
between metaphor and ear, irony and tongue.

True to chaos, you carry prisons
in your heart and denounce others
when you are the jailer that jails you.

True to form, the heart points down when sad,
up when happy, lights up an abyss and
overcomes each abyss tainted in blood.

True to chaos, I prefer passion to possession,
an earth who understands, mornings seized by joy
in the opening poppy, beyond the range of the visible.

True to form and true to chaos,
throbs of a poetic heart
cannot be reigned in by the prosaic hand.

True to chaos, gravitational collapse at the end of a star's life
creates its own chaos grid sound
in the magnetic field evolution of heavenly bodies.

True to form, Argos-eyes is no historian
since he lacks the owl of Minerva's flight
into history as past matters of fact.

True to chaos, language games us
into connecting the dots in hemispheres
of the brain and slips of the tongue in cheeks.

True to form, the why of performance
seeks reflection in another's vision
in the divinity of meeting, our shared humanity.

True to chaos, a seashell and nearby dragonflies
congregate over the next century
beginning one autumn night among friends.

True to form, the clock is always striking
when you are hungry and thirsty and you know
that you, the dreamer, have not dreamt that you are dreaming.

True to chaos, prophecy is an ingredient
in the cosmology of each covenant filled with beauty,
with ashes shaken from the rising dead.

True to form, cherry blossoms
inspire flower arrangements that reveal
eternity no further than the earth, sea and sky.

True to chaos, petrified sky melts in the crackling
of the sun and sings with the green willows
where most of us no longer try to flee the world.

True to form, love feasts have their own degrees
of chaos yet do not sound alarmed
at the sheer angles the eye's retina can take.

True to chaos, the *vita nuova* is like a quickening dance,
a sea of father-of-sapphires, that lets innocence
become forever, give birth to desire that colors poems.

True to form, solitude familiar to dancers in the flowers
outlives desecration of grasslands, crests of tsunamis,
plagues of hate, climates of terror.

True to chaos, a partial life lives under the wheels
rather than rides them
and knows only the way of blues out of each mouth of stone.

True to form, too many countries are governed by money
and corruption, by vibrations that pierce
the inner ear, when they could be governed by virtue.

True to chaos, the Tao is the source of yin-yang interaction
and time remembered on wooden wharves
that lead to all roads, not only breakers of the sea.

True to form, untalkative and sullen, you move along
silent balconies only to find deserted forenoons,
and do not realize the joys that community offers.

True to chaos, billboards gush with blood and brains
to sell a point while you forget the vision of God
in outgoing mindscapes when dawn dawns orange in the city.

True to form, history's lifeline, between living and dreaming,
winds its way past beta-particles, friends of extrasolar planets,
and Orpheus' pursuit of Eurydice.

True to chaos, memory after memories turn and turn
while walking in the woods
but quicken when they arrive at desire under the palms.

True to form, moonlight off fishing poles reflects
peach blossoms silhouetted against the Milky Way,
slopes that breathe to the full in their emptiness.

True to chaos and, pregnant again in a twinkling retrospect,
form marks its stability along the strand where it continuously
shapes those shooting star notes of words and guitars.

For an Unknown Comedian

I remember how you were
a stand down comic
whose specialty was unwise
mock-cracking
people when they were down.
When they were down,
it felt good when you could
kick them down further.

At first, it was only harmless banter
but then jealousy, even envy
prompted you to add venom
to your comedy routines.

Your friends whose only ethic
was rudeness and rantings
chuckled and urged you on.

Even now your inferior feelings
prompt you to center stage
with your lemon sliced gossip
that erodes your self-restraint.

Dali's Persistence of Memory

The barrenness of the time-
melted landscape
is what leaps out
as though we dared blunder
into a nuclear holocaust,

a metamorphosis
we can barely imagine.

But you, Salvador, have preserved
even your mustache
in your amorphous
closed-eyed limp,
stretched-out amoeba
of a self
with mouth frozen open
your tongue hanging out.
All this
after timepieces have melted,
crawled over by ants, survivors
next to take over?

We forfeited our grasp
of the earth by our own dance of death.
Even now we can see what survives
is our outclocked memory of you, o earth,
a result of our rush to madness

by way of a surreal canvas,
painted as though on fire
at the thought of our own love
of destruction.

out of time

hurrying spending harrying
slender roses dashed in exhaust fumes
hot afternoon traffic crushing puffing where
thought blurs in this world parades
catering to expectation your face lost
in lying with unending desire upon a pyre
daring that person's taste and on tires soft

that fast lane
      everybody should buy so you
         keep running
        your money burning and flaring
           fevers your own temple resonating

   stop.

         be   still

     and   know

           you can hold

       sacred

     the silence   of stars

      lakes   where the wild duck
feeds

    mountains   where a delicate aspen leaf

       verges to fall

     ponds   that do not shimmer

       with   twilights of your face

Encounter at Bourbonnais

Not far from the Kankakee River,
A French and Indian War re-enactment:
Paris duels London
For dynastic control, a quarrel in full military regalia
By overseas empires.
Decked out in bangles, loincloths, war paint,
And mustering flintlocks,
The Hurons ally themselves with the Fleur-de-Lis unfurled.
Iroquois aid the Union Jack's regiments of bright red
Along with Scottish Highlanders in kilts and pining bagpipes
And colonials attired in cotton cloth and buckskin.

Cannon bursts and rings of smoke curl through the
Fluttering poplar leaves, meadows, and stately elms.
Captured women and soldiers slumped appear
When rifle and cannon smoke rise above the line of aims.

At battle's end, the currency becomes the crown:
The threepence replaces "tu pense." Another current:
A refining descendant of Anglo-Saxon.
The tea of imperialism overtakes Bourbonic absolutism.
Names of places become memorials
For the smoked out traces of displaced peoples.

The Hurons and the Iroquois will continue to disappear,
Trading and being traded down the river.

For John Donne

Off comes
  each mistress's gown
(and lockets)
Opening your journeys
  to Jerusalem.

For God's sake
  no sadness follows
upon the heels of amour
save oughts, guilts, conceits
  of grief.

Flesh is flesh
  bone bone
the body of love
a soul's gesture
  of desire.

Dean dear, divine
  soul is the flesh's book
when love breathes
where love wakes
  and tolls the flesh.

Body's the way love
  happens long after
that other shore beckons
a first sun, remains
  of a shadow, undone.

Painting the Last Shapes of *The Call*

Triumphs of space over lilies
are poised like pianos
holding on to a darker wood.

Not just a lost cylinder in orange-fed flecks of autumn
nearly mute as Venus de Milo.
No, these shapes, turns of words, regularly return

from a color-banked winter
where ghostly assumptions on occasion thaw.
Triangles from each year bleed at the right angle.

They breakfast on hope, strike as solid
notes of wood, pastels drawn from despair's licking self
where joy is thicker than wave-purple urchins, bolder

than any heroic frottage, deeper than epic endurable blood.
Circles, too, react within the stars, unleash the food
of purple, the graves of snake-like blue, and

make an ending bed for sleepless angels.
Triumphs of lilies over space are thinner than
any text that breeds. A thigh blue with sky

yields the sexual opus of a torso's glass lineage.
Coda: invertebrate chaos in vertebrate
shapes of emptiness that outlasts death itself.

Commencement

Calendars turn but do not
have the time silence does.
An hour glass turns to begin another flow
like history's blood in red spectacles.

So we pass, so we pass
            into glass:
in one the yestereve of kingly state
in one the now-god news of late
in one tomorrow, another revolution's date.

So we pass, so we pass
            into glass:
old births in snow
new deaths in the fall
yet the silence who speaks
beareth love's all.

About the Author

Richard Alan Bunch is the author of several collections of poetry, including *Wading the Russian River* and *Santa Rosa Plums*. A native of Honolulu, he grew up in the Napa Valley. His poems have been translated into Korean, Italian, Japanese and Hindi. These poems cover a broad range from formalist to experiments in diction, form, imagery, voice, style, and so forth. His stories and plays have appeared in several venues. His poetry has appeared in *Oregon Review, Poetry New Zealand, Roanoke Review, Hurricane Review, Windsor Review, California Quarterly, River Oak Review, West Wind Review, Poetry Cornwall, White Wall Review,* and the *Hawai'i Review*. He resides with his family in northern California.

Collected Poems conveys an atmosphere that is realistic dealing with themes such as human relations, aging, war and peace, art, loss and love, spirituality, history, and nature in all its variety.

"(Bunch's) poems strike a sharp tone, as a jazz image. He speaks of the urban, rural, and eternal malaise; and joy of man."
—*Vanderbilt Divinity Review*

"*Running For Daybreak* showcases the superbly crafted poetry of Richard Alan Bunch who three times has been nominated for a Pushcart Prize, and whose work has appeared in a number of prestigious poetry and literature publications. *Running for Daybreak* is a perfect introduction to Richard's own very special approach to lyrical verse, word-smithed imagery, and emotional imagination."
—James A. Cox, *Midwest Book Review*